PRAISE FOR *HONESTLY SPEAKING*

"As the son of a journalist, I learned early on the power of clear communication. And as a senator, I was fortunate to have Andrew in my office to practice that credo. I am so pleased that Andrew has put his essential communications advice into a book that will help any reader cut through the cacophony in both their professional and personal lives to communicate well."

—**Senator Ron Wyden**

"Good communication is at the heart of leadership, and leaders at every level should be working on improving this critical skillset throughout their careers. Andrew Blotky's book offers powerful, practical tools for leveling up communication and demonstrates how authenticity, clarity, empathy, and connection can be cultivated at work and in every other aspect of our lives."

—**Ben Rattray, founder and CEO, Change.org**

"Communicating effectively in this environment requires an ever-evolving set of tools. Andrew's roadmap to meaningful conversations is an invaluable tool. These tips can be used in personal and professional settings—and everything in between!"

—**Eric Schultz, former White House Principal Deputy Press Secretary and special assistant to President Obama**

"*Honestly Speaking* has powerful, practical, and solid advice on communicating with confidence. Andrew's expertise will change the way you think about leading at work and loving those who matter most."

—**Keith Rabois, technology entrepreneur, executive, and investor, general partner, Founders Fund**

"Andrew's book provides a powerful framework for communicating, because it flips the focus away from pushing a message to connecting with those around you in more meaningful ways. It's a game changer for anyone who wants to get better at communicating."

—Caroline Fredrickson, president, American Constitution Society and author of *The Democracy Fix: How to Win the Fight for Fair Rules, Fair Courts, and Fair Elections*

"Andrew's book is filled with practical concepts and ideas on how to communicate and connect with authenticity. He highlights 'how you are perceived is how you are,' and asks us to set the right foundation for healthy communication. Reading his book will set your company's culture up for success!"

—Toni McLean, COO, Hudson Institute of Coaching

"I had the opportunity to work with Andrew for several years at Facebook during a time when both the how and the what of what leaders communicated became increasingly critical. There are useful, credible tips in here that are based on those years of experience and can help you shorten your own learning process with regards to culture, communication, and authenticity."

—Mike Rognlien, author of *This is Now Your Company: A Culture Carrier's Manifesto*

"Andrew's ability to weave the ancient practices of yoga with modern day psychology creates a powerful language for approaching our modern times."

—Janet Stone, Janet Stone Yoga

HONESTLY SPEAKING

Honestly Speaking

How the Way We Communicate Transforms Leadership, Love, and Life

ANDREW BLOTKY

WISE INK

ISBN: 978-1-63489-253-7

Library of Congress Catalog Number: 2019905461

Printed in the United States of America
First Printing: 2019

23   22   21   20   19   5   4   3   2   1

Cover design by Pete Garceau
Interior design by Kim Morehead

Wise Ink Creative Publishing
807 Broadway St. NE, Suite 46
Minneapolis, MN 55413
www.wiseink.com

To order, visit www.itascabooks.com or call 1-800-901-3480. Reseller discounts available.

For my grandmother Kathleen
and my mom and dad,
who taught me how to lead, love, and live,
and for all those throughout history who remind us
of the importance of speaking truth to power.

TABLE OF CONTENTS

INTRODUCTION

Communication is the basis of how we as humans live our lives—the ways we lead our teams, express love, and interact with the world around us. From the dawn of human existence, our ability to communicate with others and the world around us—through speech, writing, touch, and expression—has set us apart from other species in both the advances we make and the challenges we face. Communication is about seeking common ground and a mutual understanding. It's about relationships, about sharing ideas, and about learning from others around us. It happens in the town square, in living rooms, on phones, and on sofas.

Especially now, well into the twenty-first century, at a time when more means of communication and more information are more readily available to more of us than ever before, communication feels important to get right. But the irony is, despite more vehicles for creating connection with others than we've ever had, it's harder than it's ever been to find a connection and common ground with others, especially when they aren't communicating well with you.

When I worked at Facebook, there were many leaders who were good at communicating, but one in particular comes to mind. Who he is matters less than what he did that was so effective. I regularly saw him provide a simple, aspirational narrative that linked together all the work on a particular team, share a broader context about its meaning and significance in the overall history of communication and connection beyond Silicon Valley, and also be clear in what was expected of every person on the team—making sure that everyone had a role to play and that everyone's ideas and feedback were welcome. Whew. That's a lot to accomplish in a single presentation or meeting.

What made him so effective, however, were two things: first, he prepared and was very disciplined about how he communicated, because he really cared about doing it well. He was always able to make abstract ideas more real by using concrete examples, tie individual points back to a broader theme, and tie that theme back to what it means for people's everyday work. He provided direction for the organization less by giving a plan of steps and actions and a review of metrics than by providing a compelling, robust, inspiring story about what everybody was doing and why it was so meaningful to achieve.

Second, he was passionate. His enthusiasm was infectious and unscripted. He inspired confidence and people wanted to follow him. He was funny and relatable, which invited the listener to want to connect with him and with what he was saying. And it felt honest. He built a relationship with the audience and worked to help them to be receptive to what he said.

I share this example because it illustrates how communications works when it happens in a real, authentic way.

The typical way most of us communicate is to get out into the world what's going on in our heads. We think that once we've said what we have to say in the way it makes sense in our own heads or hearts, we've done the work. But that's only half of it. This first half is the content or the message, but the best message in the world won't land well unless the audience is receptive to it. And when it fails to be received by the other person, it's frustrating. We often retreat or push harder, finding less common ground and more fault with the other person, and being less receptive to the messages other people may share with us over the long run.

So there has to be something more. Leading, loving, and living are experienced through our relationship with others, and so communication is a two-part activity. It's more than just sharing or pushing information out into the world, it's broader than just delivering a message. It's about an array of styles and tactics that inform the way you share the information and how it's received by others—about how you relate to and interact with others. If something is worth sharing with another person, it's worth sharing because you think it should mean something to them. Whether you're delivering a project status update, sharing vacation pictures on Instagram, or professing love to the person you're dating, you're sharing the information because it's a necessary part of building and maintaining a relationship with the other person. That relationship might be with the employees you lead, your boss, your followers on social media, or the person you are married to.

The goal for you with what you share is to get significant overlap and alignment between what you say and how you say it—between your message and how you work to build a relationship with the audience.

Communication is a two-way interaction between you and your audience, an implicit agreement to seek some common ground. That doesn't necessarily mean 100 percent agreement, but it does mean mutual understanding. For most of us, effective two-way interactions are not a given. In any context, whether at work or in your personal life or online, the purpose of communication is to share ideas, thoughts, information, emotions, motivations, or intentions (information) with another person or people so that whoever you're speaking to feels, knows, or does something you want them to (receptivity).

The goal isn't to entirely overlap your world and my world, but to reside as comfortably and for as long as possible in the place of overlap, of common ground and mutual understanding.

- My goal
- My thought
- My feelings
- My perspective

- Your goal
- Your thought
- Your feelings
- Your perspective

Every person hears and interprets inputs slightly differently, and so *how* you say it is as important as *what* you say. The intention, tone, and feeling behind what you say, even if it's a weekly email report to your team at work, matters, because that's how you connect what's going on in your heart or mind with another person.

Being successful in achieving your goal, like the leader at Facebook I mention earlier, therefore requires building a relationship with another person where that person (or persons) is receptive to what you're saying.

And the good news early on in this book is that you have more control than you may realize over how receptive they are, and being good at communication is something everyone can do well, because we all practice it more than we may realize.

THE REAL NEWS OF THIS BOOK IS THAT COMMUNICATION IS AS MUCH ABOUT RELATIONSHIPS AS IT IS ABOUT SPEAKING.

People crave authenticity and connection, and with a little bit of effort, we can be what we seek in ourselves and in others. Not only will good communication help you stand out and be more successful in your personal and business interactions, but our survival as a species depends on it. In a world of more fake news, more noise from all directions, and more rapid-fire, short-form, cursory conversations, it's now more imperative than ever that we focus on how we all communicate with honesty, authenticity, and integrity. Doing this well truly will transform how you lead, how you love, and how you live.

We've all been on the receiving end of bad news or criticism. Sometimes we've felt we were talking at cross purposes with a colleague and couldn't figure out why or how to move forward. And we've all had to have hard conversations or deliver some bad news but felt paralyzed about how to do it—for example, delivering a performance review for an underperforming team member or rejecting a proposal for funding someone's passion project.

Maybe you've been at a wedding for a close friend and listened to toast after toast where people talked about themselves and not about the couple on their happy day.

Maybe you can remember a time when you felt hurt because your best friend stopped talking to you or said something to you that came off wrong. Most of us have been broken up with—hopefully in a conversation, not an email or a Post-it note—and heard, "It's not you, it's me."

All these situations have a couple things in common: the challenge comes ultimately from a place of fear in the speaker—a fear of dealing with their own emotions or insecurity. And all these situations, and so many others like them, could be avoided if we remembered, "It's not about me, it's about you."

When this phrase is used in a dating context, it is a cop-out, a signal that the speaker isn't comfortable dealing with, or owning, their emotions. Maybe it hurts them to hurt you, and they are trying to take on more of the blame. But it's still really about them, and there's usually much more behind those words—fear, the speaker's inability to deal with their own emotions, or simply having a hard time reflecting on themselves first. We all need to do a little more investigation to be clear about exactly what is behind those words. Behind *our* words.

We all aspire to be good leaders, partners, and friends. Our core human desire is to be heard and acknowledged by others in our lives.

THIS BOOK IS ABOUT HELPING US ALL DO EXACTLY THAT—BY PUTTING OTHERS BEFORE OURSELVES IN HOW WE COMMUNICATE.

Over the last few years, I've had scores of conversations with colleagues, friends, and family about what they struggle with in communication. Answers I heard included not listening, putting people on the spot, mansplaining, and speaking up without knowing what they're talking about or based on a knee-jerk reaction or a stereotype—and everything in between.

After thinking about these conversations, I realized that all the communications challenges really came down to two things: First, fear. Second, the communicator was always focused on himself and not the person being communicated with.

Too often, we think we've communicated by simply getting something off our chest or pushing out a message to a person or an organization. We press "send" and think we are done. But just because you've said something doesn't really mean you've *communicated* it. You may not have put in the effort to ensure that the person on the receiving end hears what you're saying in a way that continues to make the relationship and the interaction productive. It's the difference between pushing things *to* people and communing *with* them.

In a sense, we are getting in our own way because we're not first looking inside ourselves to sort out what we really think or feel, to really think about who we're talking to and how they might interpret what we say, and we are really bad at listening and empathizing with others. We aren't doing the little bit of hard but important work to be clear about what we are trying to convey, why, and to whom.

We often think that as we grow older we become wiser. But that's not true: we have to work at it. This is also the case for how we interact and communicate with each other. Only with effort and purpose do we become better and more comfortable at communicating, first with ourselves and then with others.

I've spent the majority of my adult life thinking about and working on communication. Most recently, I built and led the global employee communications team at Facebook for several years. I started my career working in the White House Office of Presidential Speechwriting and later spent several years working as a communications director in the US Congress, then building communications campaigns around judges, courts, and the law. I've worked on communications as a teacher, a student, a speechwriter, a leader, someone who helps other leaders communicate, and a person with friendships and relationships just like anybody else. Communicating is a passion, a career, and a lifelong journey.

And so I've spent the last year or two trying to boil down what I've learned, heard, seen, said, and felt, so it's easier for you—anybody who wants to be better at communicating in their lives—to do the good work of communicating and living more fully.

I realized that if I could help give some tips and structure around how people can be a little bit better at looking inside themselves and understanding their audience more deeply, they'd be far better at developing a personal narrative, making social media feel more authentic and useful, and communicating in their personal lives and at work.

The good news for anyone reading this book: I've done the hard work for you. Anyone can communicate well, and it doesn't have to be scary or hard.

WITH A BIT MORE FOCUS AND ATTENTION, YOU CAN MASTER SPEAKING HONESTLY BECAUSE YOU'LL HAVE LEARNED TO BE HONEST WITH YOURSELF FIRST.

And that's the key to making others more receptive to what you're sharing with them.

This book is meant for anyone anywhere who's ever struggled with communicating in a personal context, a professional context, and yes, even with themselves. I argue that most of the difficulty people have in communicating is that they've missed a key first step: doing the hard work of pulling themselves out of their own head and putting themselves in someone else's shoes.

A team feels inspired and motivated to do good work when communication goes well. And it goes well when people aren't left guessing about your intent or about the facts—whether it's a plan for a project at work or Thanksgiving dinner. When you know where people stand, what they are feeling and thinking, and if you're aligned on a plan, it's easier to talk through where there are differences of understanding and opinion and then move forward. Often communication problems are the greatest barrier to a team or family functioning well.

I've worked in organizations where this has gone really well, like in the example I shared at the beginning of this chapter. I've also worked in organizations where leaders weren't effective. They would announce decisions without explaining the reasoning behind them, the message or narrative wouldn't match people's own experiences, and often the people on the team didn't feel like they had a voice or an opportunity to be heard or valued. When the perceptions mattered more than the reality, trust eroded and people weren't willing to give the leader the benefit of the doubt the next time.

It also works in individual conversations. I've been in conversations where I've been given feedback in a direct, supportive way that was actionable and where I felt I had an opportunity to understand, internalize, and improve. These conversations level up everybody's game, because there's a sense that we're all in it together. But I've had many conversations that have gone the other way—where the person avoided the real issue, was vague, or passed the buck on who the feedback was really coming from and where I didn't trust the person had my best interests at heart, which made it much more confusing and eroded our working relationship. In these conversations, the messenger is just focused on pushing a message out, not cocreating a powerful working alliance with the receiver.

THE FIRST—AND REALLY ONLY—GOLDEN RULE IN COMMUNICATIONS IS THIS: IT DOESN'T MATTER WHAT YOU SAY, IT MATTERS WHAT PEOPLE HEAR.

The purpose of this book is to show you how to apply that golden rule. The good news is that it's something everybody can do. If you do it well, it will make you much more effective in your personal and professional relationships, and it will help you feel more confident and fully yourself.

Most books or trainings on communications focus on one of two areas. Either they focus on the context—how to spin and build relationships with reporters, how to own a room, how to have hard conversations with your partner, and increasingly, how to get more followers on social media—or they focus on specific tactics—good grammar, good social media strategies, what not to do, how to write a catchy headline, or how to tell a compelling story.

These books, however helpful and well-intended, miss a fundamental point, which is at the core of communicating effectively, especially in the fast-paced, attention-starved world of today: It's not about you. It's about who you're talking to. It's about relating to others and actively seeking common ground.

Most lessons on how to communicate tell us how to project ourselves, how to present ourselves in a way that we feel good about, and how to think about what we want to communicate based on what we'd want to hear and how we would hear it—as if we were talking to a mirror of ourselves.

But we need to flip the equation. We can't expect people to read our minds or hearts. To be successful, we can't keep focusing on what we want people to hear, know, feel, or do without making a strong effort to focus on what people *actually* hear.

I want to return to the key of communication: *it doesn't matter what you say, it only matters what people hear.* The key is to know your audience. Then it's a lot easier to be direct and assume the ownership over what you're trying to say.

We all need to take more ownership over understanding what people hear when we speak or write.

This is both a rational exercise and an emotional one. It's hard. But it's worth the effort. Understanding and empathizing with your audience—whether a person, a team, or a population—is crucial to achieving excellence in communicating.

Each of us, regardless of language, location, profession, or passion, has the same basic desire to be heard and acknowledged by others. There is not, and never will be, a replacement for human contact and compassion. No technology, no data, no ability to read minds, no communications trainings or tools will replace the responsibility we all hold for in-person connection and relating to each other. How we relate to each other is how we communicate—how we listen, speak, type, present, and look at each other.

So, if we want to be really good and trustworthy communicators—good leaders, good team members, good friends and partners—we all have to make sure other people feel they have been heard. And, in so doing, we will be heard as well.

———————

What happens if we don't focus on others first? When we focus on ourselves first, we get into a vicious cycle. When we ignore, flake, and avoid, we go back to the old mindset of putting ourselves first—and that won't lead to effective leadership, friendship, or love but instead will deepen old grooves in our minds that are harder and harder to break out of. Daily practice helps us see, feel, and hear better, and it becomes a lot easier over time. This is a discipline that gets so much easier as we do it and as we think first about our audience, then our purpose.

You might be asking yourself, "But isn't the problem that we spend too much time thinking about what other people think about us, and doesn't it feel less authentic and more calculating to try to be what others want us to be?"

The answer is, *Yes, and . . .*

Yes, we do spend too much time worrying about what other people think—while not really taking the time to understand why—without putting ourselves in their shoes.

And perceptions matter, but they matter only to the extent that those perceptions are things we can shape. If we understand and really empathize with those we are speaking to, communications is about a set of tools we can use so that other people hear what we want to tell them and see us in the light we want to be seen.

Empathy is the way we understand, deep down, how others can and want to be seen. Taking the time to understand others in relationships of any kind, whether at work or at home, with the person who drives the bus you ride or who pours your coffee each morning, is about connecting. The word "communication" comes from the Latin word *communicare*, which means "sharing" or "to make common"—to impart, join, unite. Communication is not a one-way street or a solitary activity. Speaking only matters if it's heard. Humans invented language and the ability to write in order to share knowledge with each other.

Empathy and connection are at the root of communications, and they have a significant impact on just about every aspect of our society today. The tools in this book will help you solve the problems you face in many contexts with developing empathy, with sharing and finding commonality through your words. Because it's not just interpersonal communication where it matters; how you convey your thoughts and connect with others around you has a significant impact where the stakes are the highest.

For example, there are many diagnoses for what was behind the surprise outcome of the 2016 presidential election, but one aspect of the campaign was really at its core the ability of Hillary Clinton and Donald Trump to relate and connect to key voters. Yes, three million more US voters nationally voted for Hillary over Trump. Nonetheless, clearly not enough voters connected with Hillary's message as strongly as they did with Trump's in a few key states. Trump communicated effectively, clearly, and convincingly with those who felt left behind and cast out and those who harbored fear and resentment—and Hillary did not, at least to the same or a greater degree.

There isn't enough space in this book to explore all the details of why the 2016 election turned out the way it did. But that campaign and election showed how much more effective simple, clear messages that inspire strong feelings of fear are than nuanced messages showing a strong command of policy and governance. It's an interesting, game-changing challenge to understand how to communicate effectively with voters in future elections. For our purposes, it shows how important it is to keep emotions in mind when communicating your message.

But why does communication matter in the workplace? For one thing, it will help you get hired—or get a raise. For another, perhaps more importantly, it's what distinguishes effective leaders. Bill Campbell, a well-known CEO coach, often shared a core leadership lesson: "Your title makes you a manager, your people make you a leader." When people are empowered to live up to their full potential, that makes you a leader. Good leaders cultivate empathy and connection with the people they work with.

Recent studies show us that employers increasingly rate "soft skills" like communications as a key competency they look for in hiring, with 77 percent in one study saying they were as important as hard skills.[1] Employers in the workplace increasingly cite communications and transparency as among the most important attributes in a company in employee engagement surveys. Salesforce reports that companies that communicate effectively are 50 percent more likely to have low employee turnover rates.[2] Companies and nonprofit organizations alike are increasingly investing in communications platforms and skills trainings for their teams because they realize how critical it is for retaining employees and achieving their objectives. When a 2015 Pew study asked respondents to select the skill that was most important for children to learn in order to succeed, 90 percent said "communication."[3]

More than any other skill, communicating effectively is at the core of leadership and love. But it's a discipline. Like anything worth doing, it takes effort. This book is about encouraging everyone to put a little more effort into communicating well—which will yield better, nicer conversations in our world—and give you some tools to make that effort easier, faster, smoother.

---

1. Harris Poll of 2,138 hiring managers and human resource professionals age eighteen and over between February 10 and March 4, 2014.
2. Leung, Stuart. "Why Interpersonal Communication Skills Matter More in Business Than Intelligence." https://www.salesforce.com/blog/2016/06/interpersonal-communication-skills-matter.html
3. Pew Research, "The Skills Americans Say Kids Need to Succeed in Life." https://www.pewresearch.org/fact-tank/2015/02/19/skills-for-success/

In these pages, we'll review some important lessons I learned while building and leading a communications team at Facebook and working with elected officials, the media, grassroots advocates, the academy, and yes, my personal life. We'll also introduce a few frameworks for helping you write, speak, and be more open and effective in communicating so that you can lead and love in a more effective and satisfying way.

Chapter 1 is about knowing yourself, being honest with yourself, and knowing your audience before you even begin communicating. In chapter 1, I also share the two key questions you should always answer in communications.

Chapter 2 is about the importance of self-reflection. So often the difficulty we have in communicating in any context comes from our lack of clarity on how we show up and want to come across. I'll talk about authenticity, fear, and how to use self-reflection to make communication easier.

Chapter 3 is about listening. Listening is at the core of connecting with others and communicating with clarity, respect, and honesty.

Chapter 4 is about about communicating at work. We'll talk about the importance of organizational culture and how communications is at the root of all cultures, and offer a simple four-part framework to help you communicate in the professional environment.

Chapter 5 is talk about communicating in your personal life. We'll introduce a similar four-part framework to help you communicate with family and friends.

Chapter 6 addresses an increasingly important and challenging context in which many of us struggle with communicating: social media. We'll talk about the good, about the challenging, and about you as both a producer and a consumer.

Finally, chapter 7 covers a few specific tools to help with common communications challenges and pulls it all together in my list of twenty-five things all good communicators do.

At the end, you'll find an Honestly Speaking Cheat Sheet, a self-reflection grid you can use to prepare for and guide your communication in life's most common situations, as well as some recommended reading if you want additional resources.

———————

This book is as much about how to communicate well as it is how to show up well in the world. How to build relationships with the world around you. It's about recognizing when you're leading with your own mental story about a situation rather than finding common ground. It's about managing conflict, leading with purpose, and loving authentically. It's about being your best self.

In short, this book is about how to communicate, which is at the root of all our interactions. The key to effective communications is to be fully yourself and to fully explore yourself so you can better relate to your audience—whether in writing or speaking, whether it's a team or your partner.

PART 1:

Communications
and Yourself

CHAPTER 1

Know Your Audience,
Know Yourself

"Great communication begins with connection.
What makes us different from one another is so much less
important than what makes us alike—we all long for acceptance
and significance. When we recognize those needs in ourselves,
we can better understand them in others, and that's when we
can set aside our judgments and just hear."
—OPRAH WINFREY

". . . Therefore, since brevity is the soul of wit,
and tediousness the limbs and outward flourishes,
I will be brief."
—SHAKESPEARE
Hamlet

I have good news for you as you begin this book, especially if communication has been a struggle for you most of your life: you are probably overthinking things. You are probably doing too much. Trying too hard. Performing more than being. Or talking too much.

Keep this in mind as you read on: **less is more.** Fewer words, fewer concepts, less presentation and pretending, less acting, and more simply being.

You've probably heard this before, but it bears repeating. Communications is a lot more than just media relations or social media. Those are two of the *contexts* in which we communicate. How you communicate—whether through in-person conversations, public speaking, writing, listening, body language, traditional media, or social media—is the core of effective leadership and functioning relationships. It's how we relate to each other.

But it's not that easy, right? Sometimes your well-intended messages are poorly received. Maybe your partner is constantly telling you that it's not what you say but how you say it that bothers them, setting off a neverending argument in which neither of you feels heard or validated. Perhaps you are "that guy" who drones on and on in meetings, knowing that you're losing your audience but feeling powerless to simply stop talking. Or maybe you're communicating a lack of care by simply remaining silent.

Our instinct when we meet a great communicator is to assume that some people just have a "gift" for communication and others just don't. But, in fact, anyone can communicate well. With a little self-control and a lot of reflection, you can improve—and quickly.

Here's some more good news: while some people do have a more effortless way of communication than others, everyone has work to do when it comes to communicating effectively.

THE WORDS PEOPLE USE AND THE WAY THEY SPEAK
TELL YOU A LOT ABOUT THEM—
IF YOU PAY ATTENTION.

GREAT LISTENERS ARE GREAT
COMMUNICATORS

To be a great writer, you must appreciate the craft in others and experience the written word as it's conveyed by other people. That same logic applies to communication. In order to be a great communicator, you must be able to actually stop and listen to what the people around you are saying.

You might be thinking, "I do that all the time!" But I would invite you to step back and think about that response. Many of us think being a good listener means hearing something that challenges you and quickly coming up with a zinger to shut it down. But in reality it means silencing your first (and maybe second and third) defensive reactions and hearing what others are trying to tell you.

Great listeners are great communicators. Why? Because they understand the fundamental principle behind this book: their communication has far less to do with their intention behind the message and far more with the way that message has been received.

If your spouse makes you dinner but the food is cold, you might say as much. But if in your tone or body language they hear "I don't appreciate you," it doesn't matter how pure your intentions were with your critique. Only when both people are engaged in healthy communication and understand the power of listening can your spouse avoid jumping to the conclusion that they are not appreciated. The act of listening without judgment might help them to hear what's actually being said, which might be a complete sentence ending with, "I'm going to nuke mine in the microwave for a minute. Want me to warm yours too?"

Becoming a good listener is not easy work. Our reactive instincts are deep-seated and difficult to control at times.

Think of your listening reflex as a muscle that must be exercised. Sometimes you'll be better at this than others, and that's okay. The good news is, you have lots of chances to practice good listening daily. I'll talk more about listening in detail in chapter 3.

IMPROVING YOUR CONNECTIONS WITH FRIENDS AND COLLEAGUES

You might feel like the work involved in overhauling your communication style, no matter the context, is overwhelming. How you communicate is who you are, and asking you to change is too much. And then to have to understand where other people are coming from too? It sounds exhausting.

It's not. It's necessary. And when it becomes innate, you will save endless amounts of time and energy.

A friend of mine and fellow yoga teacher is really good at this. He has a significant social media following and an even bigger following of students who have studied and trained with him worldwide. He's funny, sarcastic, and highly knowledgeable about yoga. But the key to his relatability is that he focuses on sharing things of interest to his students. He builds a following by sharing lots of really good, free content that's interesting, informative, and useful—and isn't done for the purpose of his own instant gratification. His focus is on improving the lives of his students, not on his own ego.

Because communication is the one constant in our lives, any communication issues we have in our personal lives can and will impact our careers. Your inability to listen to your friends will invariably mean you have issues listening to your boss and coworkers. Your long-winded emails or tendencies to talk too long on conference calls will also be difficult for your friends to manage with you.

Your own communication style isn't the only one you have to worry about. Creating a healthy working relationship with your boss and coworkers will mean taking on some of their communication issues and working through them. It's unavoidable work, both on the listening and communicating ends.

At Facebook, my job was to lead employee communications, and in that role I became a main culture leader at the company. Facebook is known for its forward-thinking work culture, and one of the most satisfying pieces of my role was telling new hires at orientation each week, "Nothing is culturally neutral. Everything—every email you send, every messenger conversation you have, every interaction you have in person—either makes the culture better or makes it worse." Every week, without fail, I could see the light bulbs going off inside the heads of people in the room—because it was about empowering people to show up and take ownership over who they were and how they interacted with others. The only real direction we ever provided on how to affect the workplace culture was to do it with respect and assuming positive intent, because it was important that people felt they could be honest, authentic, and empowered to be owners of the culture as much as any of the rest of us who had been at the company far longer.

That's true in every community too. With every way you show up, especially in the way you communicate with others, the question you should ask is how you can make your organization better.

CREATING EMPATHY AND UNDERSTANDING
OUR INTERNAL NARRATIVES

Empathy is the key to moving past some of the issues in our global culture of communication, and to really connecting with your audience. It might seem daunting to change the whole world (it is!), but you can focus on how to make yourself a more empathetic listener and communicator.

If you only look at the world through a camera or through the four corners of your phone, you're limited by your up-close read of people without a broader context. Through this lens, you're not able to see new things you may not know about them or accept their differences. In other words, you're inherently limited by your own view of the world. An optimistic, empathetic perspective will always be more successful than a self-focused, revenge-focused, winner-loser mindset.

Think about a time you received a message and instantly went into defense mode. Almost all of us can conjure up a time when a huge argument was the result of the littlest thing. I have found that most of those situations are the result of a lack of empathy in communication.

I've had to give hard feedback many times at work. Most often, the way I delivered the feedback was as important as the substance of the feedback itself. Some people were used to communicating purely online, so if I picked up the phone or tried to have an in-person conversation, they interpreted it as aggressive or jarring. Others were the other way around. Making sure—regardless of the content, regardless of the means—that I was explicit in saying the person's best interests were at heart and our team's best interests were our goal was always important to lay the foundation for what came next. In all cases, it's about the other person and their strengths, not just about the way I think they should perform a particular part of their job.

The same happens when the tables are reversed. Our brains quickly move from hearing to imposing a story to reacting. What if, the next time someone criticizes you, you stopped to think about where they were coming from before reacting? The result would likely be a calm discourse where a problem was admitted and steps were implemented to solve it.

This is also really important when you're communicating with people from backgrounds or experiences different than your own. Without empathy, without trying to understand the internal narratives and experiences that shape how people experience the world, you'll be caught in a cycle of pushing information out and not being heard in the best, fullest way possible. The good news is that you don't have to perfectly understand every other person's internal narrative; that would require some kind of superpower. But taking steps to imagine, to ask, to listen, to think about the broader context of your audience—whether it's a woman on a male-dominated team, or a person of color in a primarily white industry—can help go a long way to making sure what people hear matches with what you want them to hear.

THIS SEEKING TO UNDERSTAND BEYOND OUR OWN EXPERIENCE ONLY MAKES US MORE RELATABLE AND UNDERSTOOD BY OTHERS.

Imagine this sort of empathic reflection and reaction on a global scale. The results of more empathy, more seeking to understand, would truly change the world.

ON POSITIVITY

We love to judge and compare, and we often thrive in conflict. But this makes it much harder to communicate, because we are developing those grooves in the metaphoric gears that turn and run our communication engines (often on autopilot) all day every day.

If you look to the commonality and the light in people, you're better able to relate to others, and you can more realistically hear them and better anticipate how they need to hear what you are trying to tell them. It's all about seeing each other as more similar than we are different. If you are having a hard time communicating, chances are it's not solely an issue with the listener. Looking inside, and then looking to how you are the same, can help.

LESS IS MORE: THE TWO KEY COMMUNICATIONS QUESTIONS

I could go on and on with this chapter, but I won't. Why? Because the old adage is true: less is more.

Think about a meeting you've gone to at work where a person had to present on something that should have taken five minutes. Instead, they go off on a long, unnecessary explanation of their process, their ups and downs, and their grievances. Regardless of the reason, the message the long-winded speaker is trying to convey is lost on the crowd and is therefore, despite their best efforts, ineffective.

And let's be honest: It's also disrespectful. The twenty minutes that person wasted in the meeting could have been spent doing something productive. Multiply that by fifteen attendees, and that's a lot of missed opportunity.

There are a million nuances that go into our communication, but at work and in our personal lives, it boils down to one thing: less is more. The most effective communicators I know, even ones who I have vehemently disagreed with, have been able to distill their message into a few concise soundbites. The result of this has meant respect and admiration, if not agreement.

And that's the goal, isn't it? In the workplace or even in a marriage, we could never expect people to agree on things all the time. But they can have open dialogue about the things they disagree with, every time.

People complicate things when it comes to communication because they miss asking the two key questions everybody should always start with in any communications context:

1. **Who is my audience?**
2. **What is my purpose?**

Doing the work of answering these two questions clearly and honestly will help set you up for success in almost any context.

It takes a bit of empathy to answer the first question. The surface answer might be "my boss" or "a room full of strangers," but of course the real answer lies in how your audience communicates and being self-aware enough to know just how much information they need. A room full of salespeople don't need to know the technical background of a project, just as your spouse doesn't need you to rehash all their shortcomings before asking them to change a behavior.

Knowing your audience means respecting their time and intelligence and communicating with them in a way that they will respond to.

It takes a lot of self-awareness to answer the second question. The surface answer might be, "I want a raise" or "I want my spouse to know they hurt my feelings," but the real answer might require some serious reflection. "I operate in a vacuum in my job and don't feel like I'm seen or appreciated" might mean that the purpose of your talk with your boss is more than just asking for a raise; it's figuring out a more consistent means of communication.

You can be empathetic without being alarmist or overly emotional. Truly listening, understanding, and taking the time to explain the rationale and thinking behind their point of view in an orderly, measured way was the key to many of these leaders' success.

While working with the employees at Facebook, I found that when they didn't jump to conclusions and didn't immediately move into a defensive posture but rather took the time to understand the point of conflict and shared a point of view in a clear, direct way, often the person on the other side felt a lot better and came to a much deeper understanding of the issue they were concerned about. Even if they didn't like the outcome, the communications style could create more clarity, more shared understanding, and a greater ability to trust and collaborate in the future. They felt like they had been heard and understood and like the person valued them enough to take the time to explain and bring them along.

The table below shows three common situations that can be difficult but that, with a small shift in your language, can convey much more empathy and connection—and achieve your desired goal. Focusing the communication more on just the relevant facts and on positive intent meant for the other person, rather than simply sharing a reaction based in your own emotional state, can really help the other person hear what you're trying to tell them.

SITUATION	INSTEAD OF	TRY
You are giving a presentation at work about a project that you are having a lot of difficulty with.	"When we first started this project, I felt like we were on the right track. It's been really hard because of A, which was caused by B, and we really have tried so many things to fix it. I don't know what to do, and here is why . . ."	"Project X has these three major roadblocks: A, B, and C. Our team would like to see X implemented so we can move forward."
You feel like you are doing more than your fair share of the housework.	"You are always doing X. It makes me feel Y. I work all day, and you have more time than I do. And then to top it all off, Z! I've had enough."	"I need more help doing the dishes. How about we switch off weeks?"
An employee you manage is underperforming in some way, and you need to put them on a corrective action plan.	"You know, the team has all been feeling weird. You are good at X, but you don't really do Y very well, but you are great at Z. Do you think that maybe Q thing needs to happen?"	"I want you to succeed here and I want to help you be the best you can be at this job. However, the work you are doing on this X is inconsistent. You might consider doing A, B, and C. Can I help you with those things?"

These examples, and countless other situations like them, are really best when you cultivate within yourself a sense of empathy for the person with whom you're communicating. Getting out of your own way, getting out of your own head, and focusing on your overall goal will help ensure that the outcome is better, is less confrontational, and preserves a long-term relationship. Being direct, but with empathy, is the main goal here.

Putting these skills into practice takes work. But the good news is that cultivating this direct, concise communication style will make it much easier for you in the long run. The people in your life will know that they can trust that you won't mince words or lead them on, even if the message is a tough one, and you will save time and emotional energy by not dancing around issues that never get solved.

CHAPTER 2

The Important (and Difficult) Work of Self-Reflection

"What is it that remains essentially you?"
—LYNDA GRATTON
The 100-Year Life: Living and Working in an Age of Longevity

"Don't bother just to be better than your contemporaries or predecessors. Try to be better than yourself."
—WILLIAM FAULKNER

If you've picked up this book because you are having issues with communication in your life—with either your coworkers, your boss, your team, your spouse, or your family—I have good news for you. Many of these communications issues you're experiencing can be brought back to one unifying problem: fear. We'll talk about the role fear plays in your life later in this chapter, but keep this in mind as you read: our brains are hardwired to protect us.

Your gut reaction to a situation, particularly one having to do with communication, is to overthink, overanalyze, and overprescribe, because your instinct is to protect yourself from harm. But the truth is probably much simpler than that.

It's fear of our own emotions, fear of how others will perceive us, and fear from deep down that we aren't good enough.

SELF-REFLECTION AND UNDERSTANDING WHAT YOU REALLY MEAN WILL HELP YOU TO SHARE MORE ACCURATELY WHAT'S GOING ON INSIDE SO THAT WHAT PEOPLE HEAR IS ACTUALLY WHAT YOU WANT THEM TO HEAR.

Understanding what, exactly, you fear—especially if it's a fear of being misunderstood or a fear of disappointing someone and engaging with their reaction—will help you better manage what you say and how you say it. The simple act of acknowledging and naming your fear will help you see that it's just a creation of your mind and then give you the ability to more clearly sketch out a way forward.

Let's start with an example I think most people can relate to. Your boss pulls you aside and says she has feedback for you. Rarely do we ever think that it's something positive; we always first think, "Oh no, what did I do?"

Your knee-jerk reaction is:

- To panic. Your boss doesn't like you. She's never liked you. You made a terrible mistake getting involved in this company. Time to look for a new career.

- To cry. No one understands how hard you work. No one gets the struggles you face every day.

- To shut down. You've done the best you can but you can't possibly be expected to do more. Just let your boss drone on, zone out, and then go right back to your normal way of doing things.

- To get angry. This is so typical of your boss. She's always had it out for you, constantly picking on you. She just doesn't like you, and you're sick of it.

- To blame her, or someone else, or everybody else. It was someone else's fault, it doesn't jive with how you think you do your job, and she isn't treating you fairly.

Those visceral responses are fear-based and natural—but wrong. Instead, try to assume she's sharing constructive, helpful feedback on how you can improve.

We all need constructive feedback. We all want to get better, and we all need help getting better. But none of us can do this on our own. Constructive feedback, well delivered and well received, especially when it comes from our bosses, can be really useful not only in getting better at our jobs in a particular situation but also in becoming better professionals in all kinds of other situations.

All it takes is a little bit of self-reflection—real, honest self-reflection—to acknowledge those reactions as they come and decide to let them go. When we do that, we can get to the root of solving the problem and moving forward.

It works when we're the speaker too. Consider these examples from various work contexts, where often what people say isn't exactly what they mean:

What I say: I do all the work, but so-and-so gets all the recognition.

What I mean: I've noticed others are getting recognized without me. Can you share some feedback on how I'm doing?

What I say: I'm working too hard and too many hours for how much I'm being paid.

What I mean: I feel undervalued and overworked.

What I say: I am beginning to feel bored with my everyday tasks and find I finish my work quickly.

What I mean: I would like to take on more or different responsibility.

What I say: It's easier if I just do it all by myself.

What I mean: I'm fearful of failing.

What I say: I need us to rewrite this document before the deadline.

What I mean: I need for you to do this work before the deadline but have a hard time being direct with giving you an assignment. How can I help?

Creating a bit of discipline around thinking carefully about what you mean, feel, and want gets you at least 50 percent of the way toward better communication—simply clarifying, truly, what you want to share.

The fact that our brains are hardwired to immediately look to the negative, or to find something wrong and to push away from dealing with our emotions in a mature way, comes from a place of fear. Our brains develop stories about every situation—especially when things get challenging. These narratives may or may not be true, and we all have them. It's just how the brain works—as a survival mechanism and as an ordering mechanism to make sense of the unknown.

So chances are, if you're having a hard time communicating in any situation, it likely has to do with your inner monologue and a disconnect between your narrative and the narrative of the people you're communicating with. It's this disconnect that causes us to fear people's reactions to what we're saying, because we don't know how their monologue differs from our own.

We're scared of our own emotions, mostly because of social conditioning that says we shouldn't deal with them—especially at work. So when we hear news or feedback that is dissonant with how we see ourselves—or with how we want to present ourselves in the world—it's uncomfortable, and we aren't equipped with the tools to talk about it.

THE KEYS TO UNLOCKING CLEARER, EASIER, MORE PRODUCTIVE COMMUNICATION ARE DOING THE HARD WORK ON YOURSELF, EXAMINING AND BEING AWARE OF YOUR INNER NARRATIVE, AND FOCUSING MORE ON HOW THE PEOPLE YOU'RE COMMUNICATING WITH PERCEIVE YOU.

These things all stem from being more in touch with your emotions.

Self-reflection can take many different forms, some more formal than others. It might be as simple as catching yourself in the moment, pausing for a couple of seconds, or walking around the block for a couple of minutes to observe what you're thinking, what you're feeling, and what it's bringing up for you in a moment. It might be sitting down after the next interaction and writing a note or an email to yourself about what went well, what didn't, and what you might want to change next time. It might be writing in a journal at the end of every day, taking stock of what worked, what didn't, and how you might want to try to show up differently next time. It might be talking with a trusted friend who will be honest with you and listen to what you're saying about a situation. Sometimes simply getting the thoughts out of your head and into the world, whether on paper or through your voice, can be powerfully clarifying. At the end of this chapter, I provide three straightforward self-reflection practices you can try.

GOING SLOW TO GO FAST

Self-reflection can take time, especially if it's not a habitual way of operating for you. Taking time to digest, control a knee-jerk reaction, and respond results in better communications and outcomes every time. Trying to respond quickly can result in communicating the wrong message.

Instead of rushing, we need to be more thoughtful. Going slower and being more thoughtful often means communication will be briefer, more accurate, and more meaningful. There's a lot of elegance, control, and influence in simplicity.

TAKING THE TIME TO BE THOUGHTFUL ABOUT YOUR PURPOSE AND TO REFLECT ON WHAT YOU WANT TO SAY SAVES YOU A LOT OF TIME AND CONFUSION IN THE LONG RUN—AND LEADS TO BETTER, MORE AUTHENTIC CONNECTIONS.

A business executive friend of mine told me that, after he sends an email to many people asking for input and advice, he almost always discounts the first few emails he gets back, especially if they flood his inbox within minutes of his initial note.

Another friend told me the story of a C-level executive who broke down with a direct report when he was trying to deliver hard feedback because he was confused and unclear about what he was trying to deliver. He felt like he had to have the conversation right there and then. Resisting the urge to respond before you know what your goal is and being more thoughtful are core competencies in effective communications.

AUTHENTICITY

The word authenticity has been used so much recently that it has lost some of its true meaning. "Be your authentic self!" mantras are everywhere, but what does that even mean? And what does this have to do with communication?

The truth is it has everything to do with communication.

We all aspire to live "authentically," and that simply means to live truthfully. As ourselves. There are hundreds of books on the topic of "being yourself," but the truth is that being yourself shouldn't be terribly hard work. If it is, you're probably overthinking it.

Being authentic is hard because it means being willing to be vulnerable. It requires being brave. When you take off the mask, stop pretending or presenting, and simply focus more on just being, it means being willing to show the world and those you're communicating with your true self—which can run headlong into your conception of how you should be, or how you think others expect you to be.

There is no quick, easy way to just "be authentic"—but it's a lifelong practice of stripping away the stories, the narratives, the expectations we carry around in our heads and simply finding the confidence to be and to share just ourselves, quirks, personality, eccentricities, and all.

Have you ever been in a business presentation where a person tries to crack jokes to warm up the crowd before their presentation, but because they're so tense and uncomfortable, their jokes fall flat? They spend the rest of the time trying to recover, and the presentation goes terribly, regardless of the good content.

Compare that to a time you've seen someone effortlessly tell a joke to an audience who laughs heartily. Their presentation goes off without a hitch and the audience is left wanting more.

What you're seeing there is not good luck versus bad luck. In the first example, the presenter is trying to be someone they're not. The person telling the jokes in the first example isn't a great joke-teller, and that's okay. What they did wrong was try to be something that didn't feel authentic to themselves, and it showed. Authenticity is the root of relatability and building relationships because it's about truth and seeing commonality in others.

When I worked at Facebook, part of my job was to organize the internal company-wide meetings for employees. These were always focused on a big-picture aspect of the company, its strategy, or its culture. I spent time working with just about every senior leader in the company on prepping their presentations about their work and what they wanted employees to know. These generally fell on a spectrum of inspirational to informative, and the presenters fell on a spectrum from inspiring and captivating to dull and confusing.

Some people were organized, linear, logical thinkers and had the communication style to match. There was a step-by-step order to the way they spoke that led to a logical conclusion, even if it took a bit to get there. Others were more inspirational, engaging, and funny but less organized—meaning they had to do some work to make sure their audiences linked together all the great points they made and were so enthusiastic about. Still others were far more conversational in their approach, didn't like talking about themselves or their teams but liked using stories and examples of others, and so had to focus on letting the work and the stories inspire and inform. Some were exceptionally good at employing metaphors or linking history and other contexts together in an inspiring way. Others often talked about themselves and repeated the same stories but used them to illustrate a point and underscore a sense of humility that lent credibility and trust and empathy. But all of them were only as good as they were themselves—not trying to be someone they were not.

The presentations that went over the best were simple, inspiring, and delivered by people who were just honestly themselves. Some speakers were funny. Some were really good at being vulnerable and personal. Where we always got into trouble was when speakers would try to be someone they were not.

Mark Zuckerberg and Sheryl Sandberg, the CEO and COO of Facebook, are both very public figures. They have very different styles, and neither tries to be like the other—they simply have become better, fuller, more confident versions of themselves over time. But they both prepare for their presentations, like all good leaders do, and they are purposeful about what they are trying to convey and to whom.

We are most confident when we are simply, and only, ourselves. That's because we're not wasting energy trying to put on an act or change what comes naturally to us. When we don't waste energy trying to change ourselves or to please others, we can spend that energy on other things, like creating an amazing presentation or getting at the root of a problem in order to solve it.

What the person who effortlessly told the joke to the audience did was not rocket science. They simply knew themselves well enough to know that joke-telling was a strength of theirs. They also knew their audience well enough to know that they would receive the joke well. It worked not by a stroke of luck but because the presenter had the self-awareness to know it would.

Some people are just funnier than others. Some people command a room more than others. Trying to emulate someone else rather than just being yourself means you have to deal with your own fear and try to copy and be someone else. That takes a huge amount of energy and effort, and it isn't sustainable. The good news is, it's usually not successful—so you can stop doing it now.

SOCIAL MEDIA AND FALSE AUTHENTICITY

I'll talk about how to communicate more effectively on social media in chapter 6. But social media has an impact on how we maintain a sense of authenticity, so it is worth mentioning here. Ironically, the ease of sharing on social media has made it much more difficult for people to be totally authentic and themselves. Sure, it might seem like people are posting "real-life" snippets of their lives, sometimes on a daily basis. But don't mistake presentation with authenticity. There's an inordinate amount of pressure to present a version of one-self online. Although we have platforms to be vulnerable and authentic, we more often post touched-up photos and half-truths.

This doesn't even take into the account the pressure it puts on the receiver of the message. Social media has the power to make us feel really bad about ourselves because we are constantly comparing our lives to the filtered versions we see of others.

Sound familiar?

In my work training yoga teachers, I've found that this issue of social media and false authenticity comes up quite a bit. Hop on Instagram and see what I mean; it's full of beautiful yoga models holding advanced poses while gazing off into the distance at the setting sun. There might be a caption underneath with something profound about self-acceptance, but in reality the picture they've posted is as produced as anything you'd find in a fashion magazine. Missing are the fifty or more shots showing them failing to get into that hand-stand or makeup being applied beforehand to be sure their skin glows.

What the poster is trying to communicate—loving and accepting yourself as you are—is almost laughable in this context. It's the opposite of authenticity.

History is littered with stories of politicians who eventually failed because they were seen as inauthentic—who lied, made up stories, made up credentials, or said one thing to one person and another thing to a different audience. Triangulating, trying to be something you're not, saying different things to different audiences—it doesn't work. It especially doesn't work well in the age of social media and 24-7 news, where everyone can capture an unscripted moment in which someone says something inaccurate or inconsistent with their carefully constructed public persona.

It takes a lot of energy and focus, and it's costlier in the long run.

We all face similar authenticity problems to these yoga teachers and politicians. We have a message, and probably a good one. But we so overthink our presentation of ourselves, whether by self-imposed expectations or comparisons, that we waste energy on the wrong things. We distract ourselves and get in our own way.

While it might seem counterintuitive to the idea of being authentic all the time, the answer to this problem in communication doesn't necessarily lie in being more vulnerable. It might, but not necessarily. Living authentically doesn't mean blasting every difficulty on social media, in the same way that it doesn't mean dragging down work conversations with complaints about your personal life.

Being vulnerable, truthful, and authentic is one thing. But being vulnerable because you feel it's expected or trying to "out-vulnerable" someone else will have a negative effect on your communication.

Take this instance, for example: Imagine you open your social media app of choice and immediately see someone's long, ranting post about their bad day at work. Or a heartfelt, long post about a struggle with an illness of some sort. They are expressions of vulnerability and often, if you get down to it, a call for attention of some sort—either for support or for attention's sake.

What do you usually find below it? Often you see expressions of love, support, and affirmation for you and what you have shared. These expressions matter and they are important.

But sometimes people manipulate a communication opportunity for something that's not as real or as authentic. Sometimes these posts turn into a landslide of other posts or comments from people trying to get attention for themselves or to out-vulnerable each other. Or they see a person of influence, like their boss or a celebrity they admire, talk about a hard situation and get a lot of attention and support, real or fake, and feel that they need to do the same thing—and often get into a spiral of trying to outdo each other in the race to be "authentic" and vulnerable—for the attention it gets them, rather than the learning, feeling, or doing it calls on from their audience.

We've gotten into a situation where people excel at hurting their own feelings, taking offense at things that may not really affect them that deeply, and where it's about performing and performative emotion more than simply, truly, authentically being.

Being authentic is really valuable, and telling a true narrative about yourself is a core way of connecting to others. But pushing out narratives where everyone has a tragedy in their family, where everyone one-ups each other in how bad their days were or the commute was, actually gets away from the desired intent: rather than creating more empathy, you create more estrangement. If you're outraged about everything, can you really be outraged about anything? Rather than making sure the audience really hears what they're trying to say, people focus more on the drama around their story.

But manufactured vulnerability gets in the way of empathy because it represents a shift away from the audience and back to the speaker. It refocuses the attention back to I-me-mine and away from a meaningful connection or acknowledgment of someone else—and letting that be enough.

It even shows up when you talk to a friend or a colleague and point out something interesting or new or personally vulnerable, and she says, "Oh yeah, I already saw that." Or, "Well, that's why I work this way and did this thing, so that I wouldn't struggle with that." These small comments shift the focus from the content and the shared connection back to the person and about themselves, which kills empathy, connection, and often, the conversation. It becomes more about who knew, saw, felt, or experienced it first, and almost a competition, rather than a shared moment.

———————

How do you know when your communication style is not authentic to who you are and therefore ineffective? The answer goes back to the crucial work of self-reflection. Take some time to be curious about who you are and how you might be perceived by others. Ask for feedback, and be open to it when it comes. Self-reflection practices like we talked about earlier are really about stopping in the moment or soon afterward and being an investigator into your own situation and your own reactions. One of my friends calls this "being a scientist of your own behavior." Investigators and scientists use many different tools, but they are all seeking to understand better and more deeply. Here, this is about noticing how you're thinking and feeling and even asking others how they saw you come across and how you can get better. It's impossible for us to step out of our own bodies and see ourselves as others see us. But just as people record themselves when rehearsing for a show or a speech, asking for specific feedback about how direct, shy, hard-charging, or lighthearted you are can help you better understand the way you come off to others.

Understanding how you're perceived is a gift. It's additional data you can use—not to change how you act to adhere to someone else's idea of how you should be, but to get a fuller understanding of what you would need to do for people to hear what you want them to hear. If it matters not what you say but what people take away, you have to understand how people hear you so you can communicate accordingly.

Listen to your body. You know that feeling of nervousness you get when you are about to give a presentation on something you feel confident about? Compare that to the feeling of nervousness you get when you aren't confident in your material. One type of nervousness is good—it feels good. The other feels like dread. When you're dreading something, chances are it's not right. Maybe you're not confident in the material or the message. Maybe you haven't fully gone through the issue you want to resolve or thought about possible solutions.

Either way, your body will tell you when you are being inauthentic. When it does, listen to it. It will mean you need to take a bit more time to broaden your perspective, practice your presentation more, or maybe just smile and run the opposite direction.

You should be watching and reflecting on these habits and reactions consistently. When you're in tune with them, open to them, and actively reflecting on them, you will feel good about your material. When you feel good, your confidence will show. When your confidence shows, your intended message will have a much better chance of being received.

BUT HOW?

Hopefully, if you've gotten this far, you are open to doing some of the work of self-reflection. But you might be curious about how to best figure out who you are. The framework below can help you understand and remember what self-reflection looks like. There are really four elements to successful self-reflection and just a few parts to each. The framework in the chart that follows summarizes a lot of what we have talked about already in this chapter.

Learn	It all starts with your mindset. Are you curious, or do you already know everything? Are you sure your opinions are right? We become our thoughts, so if you only think and project fear, animosity, or anger, it infects your dreams, actions, and interactions with others. Being curious and open doesn't just mean sharing and pushing more information out; it also means being open to new ways of understanding and seeing and different opinions.
Listen	Listen to the context of situations where you feel yourself reacting on autopilot. Is this really about you? About others? Get out of your own head and just listen to how other people react to you. Watch people's body language as they talk to you. Being open and receptive is a key to self-reflection.
Empathize	Step into someone else's shoes for a moment. When that person is listening to you, what sort of impression might you be making on them? Be willing to see yourself from a new perspective and be open to whatever comes.
Connect	Ask for feedback—but not just from people you know will give you good news. Ask for feedback from people you've had communications challenges with in the past. Be open to their criticism and point of view. Ask new people in your life how they prefer to receive information and communicate.

These four elements of self-reflection should be present in any practice you use—whether journaling, emailing, conversing, meditating, or simply taking a walk and thinking. They are meant to help you develop a way of looking at how you communicate less from the lens of yourself and more from the perspective of your audience. Listening more, being in a learning mindset, and seeking to understand and connect beyond your own story and drama is the way to move from performing and pushing to more authentic, real, meaningful, and effective communication.

FEAR

Even after you've done the work of self-reflection and integrating a reflective mindset into your day-to-day experience, fear can still set in. Being yourself means being vulnerable, and being vulnerable is not easy.

So what do you do when being yourself feels too scary?

I don't have a magic solution for counteracting fear. If only it were that easy! What I do know is this: we live in a world where we have many, many chances to practice being our authentic selves, be it on social media, in a board meeting, or with our own family and friends. Every day, multiple times a day, you get to practice being you. The true you, the one that isn't operating from a place of comparison—the one that sees a problem and wants to seek a solution.

Give yourself the gift of grace. You won't be perfect all the time. That is okay. Forgive yourself, learn from your mistakes, and be willing to try authenticity again and again. The more you practice, the better at it you'll become.

And stay positive. I know, you're probably thinking about some sort of "Hang in there!" meme that shows a cat hanging from a tree branch and rolling your eyes. That's not the type of positivity I'm talking about. What I mean is this:

1. **Give yourself permission to make a mistake.** Allow yourself to fumble over a word in your correspondence with your boss. Let yourself say a few too many "umms" in your presentation. Don't get hung up on things that don't really matter. No one is perfect. Watch some of your favorite public speakers in action, and you'll see that they are imperfect too. Our imperfections make us endearing and real and therefore easier to relate to and communicate with.

2. **Adopt a growth mindset.** This means that instead of thinking things are as they are (a "fixed" mindset), you see every challenge as a chance to grow and learn and be better. This is a subtle change in your way of thinking, but it's powerful. When a problem arises and you have been tasked to solve it, or if you need someone to change a behavior or make a better choice, you are far more likely to get good results by simply assuming that the problem can and will be fixed rather than assuming nothing can be done.

Fear comes about because of something unknown or challenging. We fear things might play out differently than our minds tell us they should. We fear things that might be different than they've always been or than we think they should be. The quickest and easiest way to sabotage yourself is to let this take over. The really good news is that simply easing up on yourself, adopting a growth mindset, and widening your view to see that we all struggle with this will dispel that fear every time.

THE LONG-LASTING AUTHENTICITY MINDSET

Any work you do on self-reflection and overcoming your communications challenges should have the goal of becoming permanent. Just as a person trying to lose weight can't simply starve themselves for a month and then go back to their old habits, the same goes for living a healthy, authentic life. These habits and changes should be long-lasting. If the changes you make don't seem sustainable to you, chances are those changes aren't authentic to who you are in the first place.

This doesn't mean you get to give up when something feels hard. Sometimes the hardest and most worthwhile changes will be met with a large dose of fear and self-doubt. We've all been there, and it's easy to slip back into old habits and avoid the hard stuff.

Through building new habits that allow me to live and lead more authentically, I've learned a lot as a leader and a manager. In just about every job I've had since college, I've managed and led teams of people. I used to be really focused on how I was perceived; I wanted to be seen as a good leader, as credible, and as an adult, even though I was often the youngest person in the room.

But, over time, I found that focusing more on outward presentation and perception, rather than really connecting with the members of my teams as people, took a lot of energy and effort, and I paid the price in less close, less collaborative relationships. As the years went on, I started journaling. Simply writing for myself, focusing on aspects of the work that were challenging and the parts I was grateful for. Inevitably, most of it focused on people and my working relationships with others. But I have found that through the enforced mechanism of reflection and the practice of getting out of my own head and putting it into reality—the hard thoughts become reality when the words hit the page—I was able to tell what was real and what was just a constructed story in my own head. I also realized that in doing it more, this habit helped me to see things as less a big deal in real life than they were in my head and helped me focus more on the positive aspects of the work, the relationships, and how I show up.

Simply writing and reflecting daily resulted in improved leader survey scores when my teams shared feedback. More significantly, I was happier and less stressed because I was focused more on the work and the people rather than the constructed version of reality I was trying to live. Even though I've started my own company, I still do this just about every day. Living authentically is a lifelong journey, but simple changes in habit can help break down barriers and create more ease and clarity.

THREE SELF-REFLECTION PRACTICES

Quiet sitting and reflecting: Set a timer for five minutes. Sit quietly and close your eyes. Focus your mind on your breath alone. Notice where the breath comes from in your body. Notice the feeling through your whole body as the breath comes in and as it goes out. Focus your attention on the breath alone. Focus on your breath and your body, or focus on one of the reflection questions below.

Writing and reflecting: Get a journal. It can be of any shape, size, or type of paper. It shouldn't be a computer or electronic device. Set a timer for five or ten minutes. Either write stream-of-consciousness about what's in your mind, or select a reflection question from the list that follows and write about that.

Active reflection: Find a place outside that feels comfortable and safe, and where you can walk with relative ease and relatively uninterrupted by traffic or other disruptions for ten or fifteen minutes. As you walk, notice the context of what's around you: how the ground feels, how the environment feels, how the sky feels, how the air around you feels. Notice yourself within that context. You could also consider a question from the list below, focus on that question, and through active movement notice what comes up.

Here are some self-reflection questions you can consider, in any of the three modes:

1. What did you learn today?
2. What are you grateful for and what went well that you want to do more of today?
3. What is a commitment you want to make to yourself about how you will show up with other people at work or at home? What does that commitment look and feel like?
4. What would you do if you weren't afraid?
5. What might it look like for you to be more vulnerable with family or friends or coworkers?
6. How are you spending your time in a year, or five— what does that look like?
7. Imagine you're 90 years old, and you're writing a letter to yourself as you are today. What do you want your current self to know?
8. If you could step out of your own body, stand three feet away from yourself, and see yourself, what would you see? What shape and expression would you see? What

does that mean for you? Does it reflect how you feel inside or how you want to be received by others?

You can also use the Honestly Speaking Cheat Sheet at the end of the book to guide more specific self-reflection on your own most common communications situations.

The reality is that challenges will always be there. Again, communication is the one constant in our society, the one thing that we will always have to do. The forms of communication may change, but you will always be tasked to communicate with the people around you, and your ability to do so effectively will impact all areas of your life.

Remember this: it's about you. The challenges will come and go, the situations will vary, but that truth remains. Spending time hoping and wishing for others to change is wasted effort.

The changes you make within yourself will reverberate out to those around you. When you widen the aperture on your own lens for viewing the world, you'll be able to see situations—both problems and solutions—more clearly.

Put simply, you'll get out of your own way.

CHAPTER 3

Listening: Setting Yourself Up for Successful Communication

"The opposite of talking isn't listening.
The opposite of talking is waiting."
—FRAN LEIBOWITZ

"To listen well is as powerful a means of communication
and influence as to talk well."
—JOHN MARSHALL

If I haven't made it perfectly clear yet, it bears repeating now: the art of listening is a crucial leadership skill. It's a crucial life skill. And it's at the core of communicating with purpose, honesty, and ease. It's what ensures that people feel heard and acknowledged by others.

Listening is observing, hearing, processing, and seeking a deeper level of understanding. Listening is important as a way of learning more about your true motivations and intentions, a way of making others more receptive to you and feeling acknowledged by you, and a way that you and your audience arrive at a sense of mutual understanding. Listening is the foundation of every relationship and every interaction in your life.

Being a good listener also means others perceive you as being accessible, engaged, and responsive. They perceive you as acknowledging and hearing them, and therefore invested in them and their ideas.

We usually know when someone isn't listening to us. Especially now that we all have phones in our pockets and so many stimuli competing for our attention every day, it takes even more effort and focus to really listen and be present. Many times I've been in meetings where I've heard the voices of the people speaking but was not really listening. Sometimes I've been focused on something that just happened in the previous meeting, and sometimes I've been reacting to an email message that popped up on my phone. In those times where I simply hear and don't really listen, two things almost always happen. First, I miss out on something. Maybe small, maybe really important. But I'm missing context and facts and am not able to do my job well. Second, I make the other people feel like I think my time is more valuable than theirs and like their contributions aren't welcome.

Listening well isn't just important to a presentation or in a conversation. The same principle applies in other contexts. It can mean being more thoughtful in how you read, process, and respond to an email. Are you skimming and having a gut reaction, or are you reading, thinking, and responding?

Listening well is important because it relates back to that core desire we all have to be heard and seen—and to have some agency and choice in how we show up at work. Listening well means you are less likely to command and more likely to give a choice. Imagine, for example, an employee you work with who regularly shows up for meetings late or right on time with no time to spare. You could jump immediately into providing feedback like, "Hey, I need for you to be here fifteen minutes early, or you need to call me if you're going to be late so I don't have to wonder if you're coming." Or you could consider the other person's point of view—to listen to where she or he is coming from—and then craft a better response. Something like, "Hey, I've noticed the last few times we've had a meeting you've come in late. I'm wondering how you think that affects our work together as a team, and what you might be able to change about that?"

Listening well means you might realize the person has a reason for showing up right on time or cutting it really close. Maybe they are always coming straight from dropping off a child at school or a regular medical appointment. Whatever the reason, it doesn't matter as much as building a relationship of choice, agency, and mutual respect. You get to the same outcome but end up building a better relationship in the meantime.

Simply listening more also means you're more likely to slow down, catch important details, and give off the perception to others that you are invested in things beyond your own orbit. From the newest hire to the company CEO, being able to really listen is the key to success across the board.

Good listening is an underdeveloped, underappreciated, and underutilized skill. Get good at it, and it will make you stand out—and make you infinitely more successful.

Listening is much more than hearing. It's much more than waiting for the other person to finish talking so you can start speaking.

THE BEST LEADERS, THE BEST PARTNERS, AND THE BEST FRIENDS LISTEN. THEY ARE GENUINELY CURIOUS. THE WISE DO MUCH MORE LISTENING THAN SPEAKING.

When you listen well, you have a much higher probability of being more efficient, reducing misunderstandings, and developing empathy and an authentic connection with the person you're listening to. When you listen well, the other person feels heard. When that happens, you have assumed the power and opportunity to build a bridge with someone else, to perhaps see a blind spot you didn't know you had, and to validate the other person. It's as much about what you gain for yourself as about what you gain by being perceived as more thoughtful and more relatable.

Like it or not, we live in a world where there's a deluge of information coming at us from all angles at all times. It's not just the amount, but the volume. Everything is loud. If you have something to say, it can feel like you are screaming into the wind. I get it. Our inability to listen well has contributed to a lot of our polarization and vilification of others, and our lack of ability to be empathetic and understanding of differences in others.

Sometimes people's instinct is to talk more and louder, in an effort to at least be heard. But I have bad news about that strategy: if all you do is put opinions out there, it's a lot harder to find common ground with people and actually find solutions to problems. And the more you put out there, the more people will tune you out. The more you talk, especially if you're in a position of power, the less likely people are to feel their opinions matter and voice them—which means not only you but the entire team loses out on knowledge or different perspectives.

If all you are doing is talking—or simply waiting for someone to stop talking so you can talk—you're not listening. And listening is the key.

Every day it seems like more and more companies and public figures express opinions about things unrelated to their public persona. CEOs of just about every company—big and small—are expected to have and share opinions about any number of political issues. In a world where more people have more voice and listeners can consume those voices much more easily and widely than ever before—not just on talk radio and cable news, but any matter of social media, blogs, and videos—sharing an opinion is a way to break out, show you stand for something, and put the weight of your brand behind social issues you believe in. Whether or not this is a good thing is up for debate. I personally think it is—when done thoughtfully and selectively.

But sharing more and more opinions and sharing more loudly to compete with all the other people vying for our attention is not a winning strategy. The human brain can only process so much, and so more is definitely not better here. In fact, the opposite is true.

What I've found is that this new reality has two major downfalls:

1. Because the expectation is increasingly to reply quickly as opposed to thoughtfully, we are far too fast in forming opinions. Social media in particular is all about consumption, not about processing and digesting information. When we are simply slinging information out there to be first, we are likely missing some crucial thinking points and therefore hurting rather than helping our cause.

2. We are increasingly tribal in our forming of opinions. Check out your "friends" list on social media and see what I mean. Chances are, most of the people you surround yourself with, communicate with, and get information from are part of your echo chamber. It is not difficult in today's world to see how dangerous that can be.

It's going to feel overwhelming to try to change the culture of the world, especially as it relates to social media. It is! And that's coming from someone who encouraged some leaders at a big social media company to speak up more and more often. But that's not what I'm asking you to do.

The only thing that breaks this cycle of unhealthy communication is when each of us takes control of our own behavior and sets a positive example. The ramifications of that can be far reaching and life changing.

THE LESS YOU SAY, THE MORE LIKELY IT IS YOU'LL BE HEARD—AND OTHERS WILL TRULY LISTEN— BECAUSE THE IMPLICATION IS THAT, WHEN YOU SPEAK UP, YOU HAVE SOMETHING INTERESTING, UNIQUE, AND USEFUL TO SAY.

SHIFTING BEHAVIOR, SHIFTING YOUR MINDSET

It should be clear at this point that shifting your behaviors begins with self-reflection. Be a scientist of your own behavior by giving yourself the gift of time to unemotionally reflect on how you communicate with the people most important to you and on what you do and don't do well. Nothing will change or improve until that work is done.

But let's say you get to that part where you realize your strengths and weaknesses in communication—be it in the office, at home, or both. How do you take that knowledge and apply it?

A key point about listening is not just to hear but to process all that you're seeing, hearing, and feeling and seek to understand. When we truly listen to someone, we give up all our preconceived ideas and opinions and take time to digest their words. Putting less emphasis on good or bad, on judging and preparing a response, and instead being curious about what the other person is saying helps you keep a calmer, clearer mind and figure out how to communicate with this person even better.

Usually when we listen to a statement, we hear it as some form of an echo of ourselves. We are really just listening to our own opinion or our own experience through another person's words. If a statement agrees with our opinion or experienc, we might accept it; if it doesn't, we might reject or simply ignore it.

This is dangerous not only because we're only focusing on ourselves but also because we might grasp onto some part of the statement that's involved in our own subjective opinion—or some particular style or way the statement is expressed—rather than in the substance of it. It's hard to be good at communicating if you're always looking at things through the prism of your preconceived ideas about other people. (For example, you might think: "She's always critical of me, so I can dismiss out of hand what she's saying this time" or "He's probably going to be noncommittal and flaky again, so I'll just ignore what he says and move on.")

Really communicating clearly, effectively, and objectively—listening with curiosity and without preconceived ideas—is hard. But it's a practice, and it's important not only for your own long-term well-being but also because communicating with others is easier when they perceive you as being thoughtful and caring.

Here are three steps that will hopefully become daily habits as you work on your communications skills:

1. **Shift your attitude.** Listen to learn, not to be nice. If you're really interested in learning, not just in being nice or being perceived as listening, it will be a lot easier to quiet the agenda-setting, rapid-fire response instinct inside.

2. **Ask questions, and repeat back what you heard to ensure you understood.** This gets you some clarity and allows the other person to feel they have been heard. Studies have shown that simply asking questions, being curious, and listening to the responses make you more likable.

3. **Stop talking.** Wait for the person to finish. Fewer interruptions and more silence mean you have more time and ability to process what you're hearing, make the other person feel heard and respected, and come up with an insightful or thoughtful response. That

silence also sends a signal to others around you that you are open to new ideas and feedback, which makes you a better and more trusted leader.

If you are in a leadership position, you have a particular responsibility to do these things well and often. Is it hard? Sometimes. We all have emotions, and it's hard to squash the instinct to interrupt, react quickly, and move on to the next thing.

But I have seen it time and again: the leaders who do these things have the most productive, happiest teams. That is because doing these three things allows for trust in the leader-subordinate relationship, and trust is the foundation of a healthy relationship in general.

PROBLEM SOLVING

If you read the last section thinking, "That sounds good in theory but wouldn't work in practice," don't worry. I understand. Everyone is busy, and sometimes a person rambling or taking up too much time in a meeting needs to be cut off for efficiency. Then what? Isn't that the opposite of what I'm asking you to do?

It's really not. After all, one person taking up too much time means they dominate the conversation, which keeps other people's voices from being heard—and everybody loses out on other perspectives or opinions. As a leader, you might need to introduce some new phrases into your rotation:

"I can see we are disagreeing on this. Can we schedule a time to talk more about it later this week?"

"I appreciate all this feedback, but we are running out of time in this meeting. Can you please schedule a follow-up so we can continue this discussion?"

Listening and making more space for others is as important for a subordinate as it is for a manager, especially if you feel that your own voice is not getting a chance to be heard. It can be hard, but everyone wants to be heard. You want to be able to learn and grow, not fester in a pool of resentment. It's also helpful because the manager may not even realize they are dominating the conversation. If they are crowding you out, chances are they are doing it with other colleagues as well—so you're really helping the whole team by pointing this out.

As a subordinate, you might need to learn to say things like the following:

"I think I need a bit more time to think through my proposed solution. Can I follow up with you another time so we can talk through this more?"

"I feel like I'm not being heard. I'd like to restate the problem so everyone on the team is clear about what I'm trying to communicate."

Of course, this doesn't just apply to work situations. If you're in an argument with a friend or someone else you care about, you might want to have these phrases in your back pocket:

"Let me repeat back to you what I just heard you say. Am I understanding your feelings correctly?"

"I need some time to think through what you've just told me. Can we talk about this after dinner so I have some time to process what you've just said?"

These phrases are useful because they show you're listening and hearing the other person; you're taking some ownership over the conversation even if you feel like it's an uneven playing field; and you're speaking in a way that moves the ball forward, to a solution and to a feeling of relief and understanding.

We will talk more about how to communicate effectively at work and at home in the coming chapters, but keep this very important point in mind: learning how to listen can be a long process.

For some of us it will be easier than others. But I promise you, there is a significant reward at the end of this work. The bottom line is you are never going to get people to do what you want them to do without listening to them first, and the more you practice the skill, the easier it will become.

ON SILENCE AND "GHOSTING"

Silence can be very powerful. We often need a lack of words, of sounds, and of doing to create the space to do some self-reflection. It's also a really powerful tool in public speaking. Want people's attention? Use a well-timed pause, maybe a little longer than you think necessary, and silence will get people's attention far better, far more quickly than getting louder.

But silence can be powerful in a negative sense too. Silence in the form of "ghosting"—all of a sudden going silent after a period of communication—is one of the more harmful things we do in being better communicators.

We've all been on the receiving end of an ignored email or text message. For as annoying or hurtful as it can be for the person being ignored, it's far worse as a reflection of the character of the person doing the ignoring.

When you're in communication with someone—whether a job recruiter, a potential client, or someone you've been dating—it hurts when they suddenly stop replying to your messages or attempts to continue the conversation. It's confusing and leaves you wondering what happened and feeling disrespected. In a world of casual, consequence-free dating apps and instant messages, it's easy to not see the consequences of our ghosting.

But here's the news: the only real consequences here are in the way it reflects on the ghosters—because they've put themselves first.

Ultimately, it conveys a lack of respect for the other person, their time, and their value. It deprives the other person of that core desire we talked about at the beginning of this book—to feel heard and acknowledged by others. When you ghost, you come across as disrespectful, disorganized, or really incapable of dealing with your own feelings.

Being responsive builds trust and respect, and if you cultivate that approach to all aspects of how you exist, you'll find it much easier to resolve conflicts and find solutions.

Usually people ghost because they're "too busy" or they don't know how to respond or have the conversation. Either way, it's a poor reflection on the ghoster—because either they can't manage their work and their time effectively, or they haven't yet sorted out how to think through their feelings. They are avoiding having a conversation that might be hard to have initially but making the inevitable far harder by simply putting it off. Or they are too lazy to do either one.

The key parts to any response here are simple:

1. **Don't ignore.**
2. **Respond.** Even if you don't know the answer, respond with a simple, explicit acknowledgment.

3. **Be honest.** If you're not interested, say you're not interested. If you're not going to hire the person, say they aren't the right fit for the role. Putting it off only makes the eventual conversation harder and makes you come across far worse.

4. **If you can't reply right away, say when you think you'll be able to reply.** Doing so is respectful of the other person's time, and also gives you a self-enforcement mechanism to deal with the issue and then move on.

But the key is to reply. Rather than ignore, respond with something along these lines:

- *"Hey, I got your email. I'm in back-to-back meetings today, but I will reply by end of the week."*

- *"Hey, I got your email. We are still sorting out our hiring needs, but you're still in the running. I will follow up with you as soon as we have some clarity."*

- *"Hey, just acknowledging I got this. I need a bit of time to sort a few things out. Give me a few days. Thanks for understanding."*

All these responses keep you looking like the good guy even if you have something to say that might be disappointing to the other person.

Gandhi wrote, *"If we could change ourselves, the tendencies in the world would also change. As a man changes his own nature, so does the attitude of the world change toward him."* In other words: the more respect and responsiveness we show, the more we're likely to cultivate it in the world we inhabit—and the more connection and effective communication we're going to see.

SELF-TALK

You might not think about it much, but you are constantly talking to yourself. Not in words, per se, but in the narratives you create in your mind about everyday situations. Those narratives have the power to shape and change your life in dramatic ways.

Let me give you an example. I was recently talking with a friend about my career and the ups and downs of starting a consulting business. She mentioned that the company she worked for would love to have someone like me come in to lead their human resources team. She asked if I would be interested in a position like that.

My instant reaction was to say, "I'm not an HR person."

Almost immediately, I realized what a strange response that is. First of all, what is an "HR person?" Second, where had that instant negative reaction come from? Instead of hearing that someone thought I would be good at an important job and taking it as a compliment, or that someone was gracious enough to recommend me for a job, I heard a suggestion that I felt was outside the bounds of what I could do, or do well. I was doubting my own ability and dismissing the idea before I had even thought about what an interesting, meaningful opportunity it would be as a next career step. Everyone struggles with this in some form or another. Maybe your own negative self-talk involves not thinking you're good enough for a job or a person.

A coaching client of mine, who is now a very accomplished professional, recently told me a story about how he didn't apply for his dream job because he was scared that he'd be found out not to be as good as he thought he was. He was scared to even get into an interview situation because, while he wanted the job and thought he could do it well, he was intimidated and let the negative voices inside his head talk him out of being able to interview. He was his own worst enemy because he allowed the negative voices in his head to run out the clock.

Part of being a scientist of your behavior means being able to step outside your own head and recognize your habits and instincts without judgment. This means accepting that those negative thoughts are indeed hardwired and will take work to overcome. The next step is to start using some of the tactics we've already discussed to overcome some of these negative habits.

1. **Notice your knee-jerk reactions to situations, particularly ones where you are challenged.** Are you quick to find a reason to shoot down people's opinions? Are you constantly interrupting people and not letting them finish their train of thought? Instead of listening, are you searching for the next thing to say?

2. **Develop a forward-thinking mindset in a way that feels authentic to you.** For some people this will mean writing in a gratitude journal, and for others this will mean incorporating some sort of meditation into their daily routine or constantly reminding themselves that going to a negative space isn't serving them in any way. Lots of books, like *The Power of Habit* by Charles Duhigg, show us that one positive change can reverberate in other parts of your life. I talked about

journaling daily in an earlier chapter, and the simple act of writing out my thoughts about work and challenges with projects opened up entire new, richer, more authentic ways of connecting with people in a variety of aspects of my life.

3. **Give yourself the gift of grace by allowing yourself to make, correct, and move on from mistakes.** No one is perfect all the time, and you are no exception. Some days you'll be better at positivity than others, and that is okay. The good news is that you have each and every day of your life to improve upon this.

4. **When in doubt, listen with curiosity and an open mind.** Yes, I'm saying this again, because it's really that important. When you find yourself spiraling into negative self-talk about yourself, the people in your life, or your situation, stop and listen. Don't do anything beyond that. The simple act of listening will open up your perspective and allow for more understanding, empathy, and compassion, which will in turn make all your communications more rewarding and fruitful.

Negative self-talk is one of the most powerful inhibitors to good communication, and it's entirely within our control. Simply recognizing when it happens, stepping back, and observing it rather than following its every twist and turn can really help you be clear about what your overall, bigger purpose is and how you should communicate with your audience. Self-talk is automatic—our minds love to develop negative or defeating narratives. Listening to that talk track and then simply putting it aside can work wonders in all kinds of situations so you see more clearly the factors in front of you and how to communicate with others around you.

KNOWING WHEN THE TIME IS RIGHT

Hopefully by this point you've come to understand the value of listening and reflecting. You might have been nodding along with each paragraph, agreeing that for day-to-day problems with quick solutions, these strategies are probably a good idea.

But what about those times when you know that communication needs to happen but will be difficult? What do you do when you know that you're treading into murky waters, and despite all your best efforts, there will probably be some fallout from the message you need to give or receive?

Whether this is the first, second, or third time you're reading this book, chances are that you are refreshing your memory because you are currently in a situation requiring some sort of delicate communication.

In the coming chapters, we will be discussing how to implement these practices into your daily life in work and at home, but before we do that, we need to talk about how to know when to have those hard conversations.

It should be obvious at this point that there's no one-size-fits-all when it comes to communication. It's the one constant in our lives, the key to our success and overall happiness. So yes, part of the answer to the question of when you should have hard conversations lies in trusting your gut. The work you do around self-reflection will be immensely helpful in this.

What I can tell you is that before you move forward with having a difficult conversation in work or in life, asking yourself these three questions will help you decide whether or not the time is right.

1. **Am I doing this to get a reaction?** Think about the last time you posted something on social media. The last time you blurted out something in a staff meeting. The last time you challenged your spouse, your local politician, or a friend at a dinner party. The last time you texted a person you were interested in one or two too many times. Were you hoping to make the person uncomfortable in some way? Were you trying to show off in front of someone else? Were you trying simply to get a text back? If the answers to those questions are *yes*, apply that knowledge to your current situation. If your goal is simply to get a reaction, chances are the "issue" you are bringing up might not be worth the expense of energy and time.

2. **Are you looking for short-term validation?** Think about your goals for this communication. Are you hoping for a quick pat on the back? A laugh? Are you trying to make sure that the people you report to see how hard you work? Are you being passive-aggressive in trying to get validation? If the answer to any of those questions is yes, consider the problem from the lens of nonattachment. Short-term validation will mean short-term reward, and the goal for your communications should be long-term change and happiness.

3. **Are you looking to move things forward?** Many of us have worked with (or been) "that guy," the person whose sole contribution in meetings is to shoot down ideas or offer unhelpful anecdotes, draining all the energy in the room. This habit can be broken by having the self-awareness to ask yourself if what you are adding to the conversation is moving things forward or not. Of course it is sometimes important to add a dissenting opinion, but keep in mind that to disagree should also involve adding an option to move forward. Similarly, having a tough conversation with a boss, spouse, or friend about something that's bothering you will go much better if you have a plan in place for how to make things better rather than simply complaining and leaving it to everyone else to figure out a solution.

PART 2:

Frameworks
for Successful
Communication

CHAPTER 4

Effective Communication at Work

"I think the one lesson I have learned is that there is no substitute for paying attention."
—DIANE SAWYER

"I have made this letter longer because I did not have time to make it shorter."
—BLAISE PASCAL

There's a saying in business I've heard in a few different circles, often attributed to management guru Peter Drucker: "Culture eats strategy for lunch." It means, in essence, that your workplace could have the most incredible business strategy in the world, but if your company culture is toxic—if people are unheard, unappreciated, and unhappy, or if it feels incongruent with the mission of the company itself—the business won't be successful.

In your place of work, strategy is constantly changing. Business goals, management, investments . . . all those things can change, and often. But culture is much, much harder to change.

Culture is the sum of how people feel. Culture is the way we work—the collective total of the actions and behaviors related to how we get our work done. Usually, cultures are guided by some shared set of norms, values, or work principles—which all have to be communicated, shared, and lived every day. But you can't change how a person feels just by delegating it on a spreadsheet.

This is why the work I do with leaders is so critical. Of course CEOs are looking out for the bottom line—that is their job. But reaching that goal simply won't happen if the team doesn't feel supported, included, and safe.

Every leader can and should excel at communications. Organizations and cultures are rooted in communication. In the professional context, good communications is a combination of information sharing and culture guiding. It's about making sure people have the information they need and a clear set of expectations about how to do their jobs.

As a leader, really good communication means that the people you work with—your team, your broader organization, and your partners—have the information they need to do their jobs, have a clear sense for where the organization is heading, and feel part of a good culture. It's done through clear, consistent, substantive **messages** that are distributed through a variety of well-functioning **channels** for distributing information and gathering feedback.

Think of the messages as the *what*—the substance of what you're conveying and the tone and style with which you convey it. The message could be an announcement about a new product launch, a new policy position, a new way of running a process, or a new aspirational goal. What are the facts? *What* is also the tone and intent with which you communicate. Do you want someone to do something? To know something? To feel a certain way?

Think of the channels as the *how*—the *where* and *by what means*. Where are you sharing the message? Is it through an in-person conversation or a meeting? Or is it a longer presentation? The complexity and purpose of your message will help determine which channel is best and where to share it.

Being clear about your message and your channels requires understanding your audience, how they process information, their level of knowledge or sophistication, and what you want them to know, do, or feel.

The work around creating a healthy communication environment is much more than a feel-good exercise; it's downright crucial to getting things done and being successful.

Communication is the way cultures live and breathe. It is the way people develop and maintain the patterns of behavior that define a culture. Culture is really about how people interact and whether they feel a sense of fairness, safety, and control. Our core desire to be acknowledged and valued matters now more than ever, especially at work.

CULTURE AND YOU

No matter what your level is at your company or how big that company is, it is imperative that you understand the important point: nothing is culturally neutral.

Especially around communications, this is really important. At a lot of companies now, people communicate increasingly through web-based chat and intranet tools—in addition to email, phone, and in-person conversations. When I was at Facebook, I helped create the version of Facebook for use specifically inside companies—something now called Workplace. Workplace came about based on how we used Facebook within Facebook for Facebook business. Specifically, how we used Facebook groups to share information, collaborate, and get work done.

Every post and comment in the vast majority of groups is public and visible. They set the tone for how people communicate more broadly. A culture based on open, transparent communication and real-time feedback works well when people are direct but empathetic and assume best intent. Those same tools don't work as well when people are direct to the point of being rude or bullying. A seemingly small, innocuous question taken as a comment or a criticism rather than as an actual inquiry can make the culture better or worse, because people take their cues from the behavior they observe in others. This is especially true if those they observe are in a position of power or authority or are a culture carrier within the organization. From implementing Workplace—both at Facebook and in many hundreds of companies globally—we learned that the real value of easy-to-use, open, transparent tools is only as good as the cultural norms, behaviors, and ways of using those tools. The more open, collaborative, and simultaneously direct yet supportive people are, the better the tools work and the better the business outcomes. In short, the best communications cultures are ones that have a blend of good tools and good behaviors. One without the other won't work well.

Everything you do—every email you send, every meeting you lead, every interaction that you have with others—makes the culture better or makes it worse. At a larger scale, the impact of those small actions each of us takes, when work is easy and when it's stressful, add up to big changes and really powerful patterns. That means that you—no matter your role or how long you've been in an organization—are 100 percent responsible for creating the culture at your place of work. Not sometimes, but all the time. Every day.

YOU—YES, YOU—ARE RESPONSIBLE FOR MAKING THE CULTURE OF YOUR ORGANIZATION WHAT IT IS.

This is a powerful realization and should have a dramatic impact on how you communicate at work. Your role likely relies on communication, both internal and external, all day, every day. In each and every one of those moments, you are impacting your work culture.

Notice that I didn't say you "have the chance to" or "are empowered to" impact culture.

You *are* impacting culture. In everything you say or do, along with everything you don't say or do.

This should be liberating. It means the power is in your hands and in your words. It means that all the reflection work you have done in previous chapters will impact the lives of the people around you as well as your company's bottom line. No matter who you are or what your pay grade. No matter the type of community or organization you're a part of.

A KEY POINT OF IMPACTING CULTURE AS A LEADER IS TO REMEMBER THAT THE INTERACTIONS YOU HAVE AREN'T ALWAYS ABOUT WINNING. IT'S NOT ABOUT WHO'S RIGHT AND WHO'S WRONG. RATHER, IT'S ABOUT GROWING AND IMPROVING.

The most effective managers and leaders elevate the debate. They widen the aperture and keep a focus on the big picture. Whether it's in a feedback session, a big internal debate about strategy, or a major moment of crisis, the best leaders focus less on "being right" in the moment and winning the argument and more on conveying empathy and care. They push people to get better together.

So how do you know if your company's culture is set up for success?

In my experience, healthy work cultures can look different, in the same way that two perfectly healthy relationships might not look the same. But across the board, the healthiest work cultures put the following communications strategies into regular practice:

- **They are constantly soliciting—and listening to—feedback that's based on people's, or the organization's, strengths.** It can come from surveys, one-on-one meetings, mentoring sessions, open forum sessions, or some combination of all four. A culture of feedback means people are invested in the outcome of the work and are empowered to share their views because they trust they will be heard. This is more than simply showing that management is open to feedback (though that is important). It shows that there is open, honest communication happening regularly. This is the type of organization you want to work for.

- **They are inclusive. Lots of companies pay lip service to diversity and to having a "supportive" culture, but this is a bit trickier to put into practice than you might think.** Support means making each and every person on the payroll feel valued and appreciated. It means making sure people with different backgrounds and perspectives like women and underrepresented groups are included and serve as full, active leaders of the organization. Leaders that make an active effort to ensure people on their teams feel valued, recognized, and empowered to succeed create cultures where everyone ups their game and feels ownership over the greater good.

- **They don't rely solely on formal reviews to evaluate work.** This might seem counterintuitive, but the once-per-year, formal review structure is not conducive to a healthy work culture. Think about it: do you really want to work somewhere that only listens to what you have to say once per year? Healthy communication needs to be practiced regularly in order to be effective. Once per year just doesn't cut it.

- **Their leadership is open and transparent.** We've all seen leaders in companies who wear masks. It's obvious from the way they talk to you that they're not listening; they're simply nodding, waiting for you to stop talking, and trying to move forward with their own agenda. A leader like this is practically guaranteed to have a team that is untrusting and unmotivated. Leadership teams get results when they are authentic and willing to move slower in order to really listen and hear the people working for them.

These points are important because they are neither static nor aspirational. They are not ideas; they are actions. Without actions, cultures are just ideas or goals that do not exist in the reality of shared experiences. Words only matter when they are backed up by actions. These aspects of a healthy communications culture are based on the idea that everybody—no matter how new or long-tenured—plays a role here. People who are new to an organization take their cues from the behaviors they observe more than just the words they hear—so if they see a culture based on open, direct, supportive feedback on all levels, they will perpetuate that culture.

The starting point in evaluating your work culture is taking an honest look at the people around you. (If you work in a huge company, focus on the team you do most of your work with.) Do they seem happy, engaged, and excited to learn? Do they express a desire to be heard more? Are they motivated? Do they take initiative, or do they do the bare minimum? Do they share direct feedback and try to make positive change, or do they complain to their colleagues and feel like they've solved the problem simply by venting?

People who are intimidated or silenced don't care about their work or the company they represent. No matter how amazing your company "mission" might be or how fantastic your strategy for a certain initiative or project, unhappy people will not produce results.

You might not need to look much further than the leader of your group or organization to get a true sense of the corporate culture. Do you see someone who is down-to-earth, approachable, and good at listening and receiving feedback? We can intuit this fairly well on a daily basis in all our interactions, and it's the same with leadership.

Changing work culture is rarely about wholesale change. To improve culture, take the things that already work well and amplify them. Any changes will be around structure and implementation and should feel organic to who you already are. Put simply: do more of what's working well, and do less of what's not.

Maybe it's added or more structured one-on-one meetings with your team members so you get more regular time for feedback. Maybe it's a weekly update you share with the team on your work and its impact. Maybe it's simply mentioning in an email you're sending to the team that you appreciate and are open to any and all feedback. Maybe it's simply listening more in a meeting and calling out your colleague for her good idea.

The other good news here is that small steps add up to big change and impact.

TEXT VS. IN-PERSON COMMUNICATION

Before we move on to a framework for communicating at work, I want to stress something very important:

WHENEVER POSSIBLE, IT'S BEST TO HAVE IN-PERSON COMMUNICATION.

That means talking to someone face-to-face or, if that's not an option, picking up your phone for a chat. Yes, I realize this can be challenging in a world based on text communication through social media, messaging, and email. People are more wedded to their phones and laptops than ever before. But none of us have to leap too far to think of a time when an aggressive comment on a social media post caused undue hurt feelings or an email was taken the wrong way.

Whenever possible, communicate in person. Especially at work, where it's easy to make excuses to hide behind your computer screen.

In-person communication is usually preferable because it's easier to cultivate empathy and connection with someone when you can look at them face-to-face and hear the tone of their voice. It's also easier to assume best intent, talk through areas of confusion, and see whether people are hearing what you're saying in the way you intend. On the other hand, it's easier to be an asshole to someone by email than to their face.

Email and text can be great for sharing detailed information or laying out longer facts and context that might be needed to make a decision. If a message doesn't require a response or a conversation, email and text might be better.

But if your message would require a conversation—or if the email back-and-forth becomes more like a conversation—generally, talking on the phone or in person is better and quicker and results in better outcomes.

Working exclusively online makes it harder and harder for us to develop connection with others and do our best to make sure people feel heard and acknowledged—the core desire we all have that we talked about earlier. It's also harder for us to deal with the fear we have of our own emotions and the reactions of others, so instead we simply hide behind an email or text and ignore the reaction it causes. Working exclusively online makes it harder for us to curb our own habits of knee-jerk reactions and to provide more thoughtful, simpler, clearer communications. Writing is a great tool to clarify your thoughts as you develop them. But relying solely on writing leaves too much up for interpretation—and at risk for being misinterpreted.

Of course, having in-person conversations all the time will not always be possible or even practical. But in the times when it is possible, do it. It will mean that when you do have to communicate via email, no one will doubt your intentions or sincerity. They will already know who you are, because you've already shown them.

Remember, it's not about you: it's about them. How you are perceived is how you are. Take the time to set the foundation for healthy communication, and that means not hiding behind email or text.

CORE: A FRAMEWORK FOR COMMUNICATING AT WORK

So you've done all that important self-reflection. You've answered the two key questions about your audience and your purpose. You know what you do well and what could be improved, and you're ready to implement some healthy communication at your workplace. But how do you do it?

Simple. In all my work over the years helping leaders and teams get better at communicating inside their organizations, I've come up with the following framework to keep you focused and on track. The best communicators follow the CORE framework: they are **consistent, open, real,** and **educational.**

I developed this framework based on my years of experience advising politicians, grassroots advocates, academics, and corporate leaders and distilling it into the most critical parts that are broadly applicable to everyone in a contemporary workplace, across industry and level. The CORE framework is meant to be intuitive, easy to remember, and easy to apply to your own style and circumstances. In a sense, these are the core, foundational aspects of effective communication at work that support the type of open, inclusive culture where everybody thrives. Following the CORE framework will help in all work contexts, and you can use it as a checklist when you're about to communicate anything in a workplace.

CONSISTENT

At Facebook, we used to have lots of leaders update their teams on their progress regularly. This became super important as the company grew and teams became larger and spread across more locations. The best leaders I worked with did this in a very consistent way: short, regular updates that followed the same format at the same time each week. They followed a similar structure and were used as an opportunity to share information, solicit feedback, show some thought leadership connecting dots at a higher level, and recognize people for something that went well. The feedback from employees was positive. People appreciated the transparency and it drove higher engagement scores internally. Simple to do, big impact.

The people around you should be able to rely on consistency in what they hear from you and how they hear it. This builds trust, particularly in our current, global way of doing things. Strategies, approaches, and business itself are constantly changing, but if you are constantly changing, people will spend more time trying to figure out how you're saying something than what you're saying.

The good news is that when you are operating honestly and authentically, being consistent will be easy and organic. You won't spend tons of time trying to come up with a new format or trying to be witty. When you build a pattern of doing things a certain way, your messages will break through easily. It will also save you a ton of time and energy when your team grows or changes. You won't be worried about reinventing the wheel all the time; you'll simply keep on doing what you're doing in a way people can expect from you.

Being consistent means both in terms of style (how you communicate) and in terms of your timing.

> BEING CONSISTENT MEANS PEOPLE FOCUS MORE ON WHAT YOU'RE SAYING THAN ON HOW YOU SAY IT EACH TIME.

Especially if you're communicating with a team or organization you're leading, reach out and communicate at regular, predictable intervals. Make sure they look and sound the same.

Consistency also involves repetition. Repetition isn't bad, especially if you really want people to internalize information and understand a theme. Conventional wisdom says that you need to say the same thing at least three times before it sinks in, so what may feel repetitive to you may not feel that way to the audience. With lots of other information competing for people's attention, especially in growing and changing organizations, memories and attention spans are short, so repeat key messages and themes so people hear what you want them to hear.

OPEN

One of my consulting clients, a big company that was family-run for years before becoming much larger, recently underwent an evolution of their entire brand—from the inside out. They started focusing on codifying their values and internal culture—both defining what they were and defining how the company aspired to be as they grew. As part of their process, they pulled together all the directors and managers in the organization for a leadership workshop focused on their culture and values to get feedback on the way they were currently defined and to gather ideas for how to implement their values with their teams.

To me, this is a perfect example of being open. Rather than presenting their plan as a done deal, they were transparent about the purpose for the change, actively sought input and feedback before making it known externally, and built ownership of the culture among the leadership team.

This is probably the most important concept in how to communicate: be open in how much you share, receive, and take in.

BEING OPEN DIRECTLY IMPACTS HOW RELATABLE YOU ARE, WHICH HELPS DETERMINE HOW LIKELY PEOPLE ARE TO FOLLOW YOU WHEN THEY HAVE THE CHOICE NOT TO.

The first necessary part of being open is being transparent with all your knowledge. You know that person on the team who seems to withhold information so they can whip it out at a time when they'll look like the hero? Don't be that person. Operating from this sense of "knowledge is power" destroys trust and makes people feel uncomfortable. Other teams need to know what you do and how you do it, and this goes from the CEO of the company all the way down to the newest hire.

"Being open" also means being open-minded. People say they're open-minded all the time, but truly walking the walk is something different. You must be open to new and different ways of doing things and constantly listen for new perspectives. You must also be aware of your biases—both conscious and unconscious—and be willing to see when your way and your ideas aren't the right or the only ones. Being open means making an effort to make people feel heard and seen.

A few specific tips on how to be open:

- **Be personal.** Don't try to be someone you're not. If you're not funny, don't try to be funny. Don't emulate someone else just because you think they are magnetic or popular or successful. People really respond to people they see as comfortable in their own skin, not people trying to fit in somebody else's. Being personal and relatable also means being vulnerable and honest. Does this mean you have to share your deepest, darkest secrets and share everything you did every weekend? No. But it means that people will see you as more fully human if you let them see that you're imperfect just like everybody else. It also means sharing your own perspective and opinion on an event, a trend, or a challenge. Doing so builds trust. Sharing stories and anecdotes and your personal perspective means you're open and inviting others to be more open with you, which is where progress happens.

- **Internal before external.** Especially now, in the social media age where news and information spread faster than ever, people you work with should have an expectation that they will hear about company matters from you rather than the newspaper or internet. Especially if you're communicating a change that may be hard or unpopular, part of being open means talking about it internally before you go outside with it. Doing this gives you the opportunity to get feedback from the people most likely to understand and support you (your fellow teammates), prepare for public feedback, and refine and practice your broader messages before going public. While confidentiality is important within an organization, and leaks can be harmful, sharing information within the team and organization means you can maintain a culture of openness and transparency, which makes people feel more like owners.

- **Feedback is a gift.** At Facebook, we built an initiative internally around this saying. It can mean different things to different people, especially if the feedback feels like a gift we didn't ask for, or want. But feedback—asking for it and receiving it openly—is a key part of how we all get better, both at what we're working on and how we work together. To be most effective as a leader, root your communications in feedback, inviting it explicitly with instruction for what you want feedback on, where you want people to give it, and how it will be most useful to you. Often the feedback you get helps you figure out what point you're trying to make. When delivering feedback, focus on building trust and rapport with the person you're sharing it with, and consider feedback focused on their strengths and what will make them successful in the long run.

- **Enthusiasm:** Being enthusiastic doesn't mean being a cheerleader or being fake. It means being excited about your work and your team's work. Enthusiasm is infectious and inspirational. If you aren't enthusiastic about the thing you're in charge of, how can you realistically expect anyone else to be excited about it? This is your opportunity to convey passion and excitement about something and, in so doing, convey to others why they should care. If you're constantly uninspired or flatlined, it's hard for people to judge whether you care and whether they should be inspired to follow you.

- **Internationalize.** Part of being open and making sure people hear what you want to tell them is saying it in ways that are comprehensible by people from different backgrounds, cultural and professional. In a lot of organizations, people use jargon or words that are barely even English. Remember, sometimes you'll be working with people for whom English isn't a first language, or for whom it is but who learned different words and terms. Make sure to be simple and clear—shorter sentences, one point per sentence.

REAL

Being real means being honest and direct. Too often in the corporate world and especially in government bureaucracies, people try to spin their words to sound how they think they should sound rather than just being direct. In the world we live in today, people have a real aversion to BS and are highly attuned to when others sound too calculating, too fake, or too political.

IF YOU WANT TO BE A LEADER WHO INSPIRES OR AN EMPLOYEE WHO PEOPLE TRUST, JUST BE DIRECT AND HONEST. IT WORKS EVERY TIME, AND THE MORE YOU DO IT, THE EASIER IT BECOMES.

This comes up in almost every work context, but perhaps a better context we can all relate to is when it happens in politics. When I worked in the US Senate as a communications staffer, it was incredible (and at times incredibly disturbing) to see how many politicians listen to their staff, lobbyists, and public polling data to determine what to say on any given issue. I worked for Senator Wyden from Oregon, and one of the things I always admired about him was that he was always direct and honest, especially with constituents. He spent time holding town hall forums in person in each of Oregon's thirty-six counties each year. I am convinced that those open conversations with people across the political spectrum and the relationships he built over time meant he only ever could be real. And it's served him well. He's been in Congress as long as I've been alive.

Too often, leaders—in politics and in industries of any kind—become masters of "spin" and say things they think their audience wants to hear, which in turn becomes complex, convoluted, hard to follow, and inconsistent over time. It becomes performing more than authentic speaking. And it filters rapidly down into those working within the organization at all levels. People take their cues on how to behave from their leaders.

Being real and authentic is so much of the currency of getting elected—we all want to vote for a person who we can identify with and who isn't fake or simply saying things to get elected. It's like that in every work context, we want to trust what people say and trust that they are being true to who they are.

To achieve that kind of real, direct communication, try adding these strategies to your everyday communications:

- **Be direct.** No spin, and no generic corporate jargon. Don't include too much context or too many justifications or nine-point plans. Just be honest and direct. Put the main point in your first sentence or two, and then give the relevant (and only the relevant) context for what you're communicating. For example, if there were three takeaways from a leadership retreat to share with your team, say that—exactly that—and then share each briefly. You don't need to go into the context behind where the retreat was, what the agenda was, who said what to whom . . . just share the takeaways in a direct, simple form. You'd be surprised how obvious but rare it is to start an email or a meeting by saying: "Today I want to share three updates about our new strategy," or "Tomorrow we're announcing a change to our benefits policy, and here's what you need to know." Just get right out and say it without using lots of flowery language. It makes the audience hear what you really need them to hear without risking leaving them confused, and actually makes it much easier, especially over time, to just say and share what you need to.

- **Be simple.** Try to have one point, or at most two points, per communication. Don't make it harder on yourself and on your audience by cramming too much into one communication, whether it's a speech, presentation, meeting, or written announcement. If you have too many pillars, frameworks, and takeaways, people get confused. A five-part strategy, with four pillars and a nine-point plan for each, is dizzying. These multi-tiered plans are why people feel like corporate speak isn't direct and trustworthy. Groups of three are easy for people to remember—pairs and single things even easier. Especially when you are speaking, try to be simple and direct. Think: if you asked someone a week after hearing your presentation what it was about, what are the one or two points you'd want them to remember? If you can say them in one sentence, do—and then start writing or creating your presentation or announcement.

- **Be purposeful.** People are busy, with an overwhelming amount of information competing for their attention and focus. If you're going to add to their information overload already, make sure you have something new and interesting to say. Don't just talk to talk. Offer a fresh perspective, a new voice, or some new facts to the conversation. You don't need to "Reply All" just to tell people you read the email or to repeat what others have said. Be intentional and purposeful—and be disciplined enough to know for yourself what your purpose is.

- **Call to action.** Often it's helpful to include a call to action. This is something you want people to do after they hear your message. This makes your intention clear and underscores what you want them to take away from the presentation. If you don't include a call to action, you risk listeners coming to their own interpretation. It also makes people feel included—so you're not just talking at them. It helps direct their thoughts and ideas into impact and outcomes. (This, again, is why it's so important to think about the objective you're trying to achieve up front.)

- **Altitude.** Part of being direct is flying at the right altitude. This means communicating with the right level of detail and the right tone for the audience you're speaking to. For a company-level announcement, fewer details are necessary than for a team-level announcement. To find the right altitude, it's important to understand your audience and ask: "What do they need to know in order to do their job?" You don't need a ton of context—just enough that the substance of what you're sharing makes sense. It doesn't matter that you know a lot more and have spent a ton of time working on something; again, it only matters what people hear. They only need to know enough to get the point, not the entire process you went through to get there.

When I created and delivered related trainings at Facebook, my audience was frequently engineers. This was because many of the engineers wanted to get better at communications as a core leadership competency, and written or verbal communications in the workplace had not been a primary focus of their training. Because of their training, many engineers are logical and direct, sometimes to a fault, and so direct communication is almost always best for them. However, not everyone can be—or should be—as direct or data-reliant as an engineer. And when you're on the receiving end of direct, blunt communication, it can sometimes feel harsh or bad and result in unintended consequences.

So what "direct" really means is to be real—to be who you are, and just who you are—and to communicate in all forms like you were having an in-person conversation.

Yes, we should all be clear and honest in our communications—but understanding your audience as well as yourself is of the utmost importance.

However you communicate, it should be authentic, whatever that means to you and your team. Be real. Don't sugarcoat, don't obfuscate, and don't deliver the feedback sandwich, where you bury the actual constructive feedback between two pieces of bland positive feedback, which are probably not totally genuine or useful.

EDUCATIONAL

Most people want to get better and learn something in their job. We all want to learn and improve. The best leaders are conscious of teaching their team things they might not already know and explaining why they might matter to them. Good leaders don't just manage tasks; they inspire their teams and broaden their thinking.

But this doesn't just apply to executive management. No matter what your level at your company, you have unique experiences and insight to add to the conversation. If you are part of a team, you aren't just a student. You're a teacher too.

As a leader, your communication should be educational and not extraneous. Your audience should learn something from it, and there should be some greater value or purpose behind it. This is important because if it's unclear or you do not share what you're intending your audience to learn or know, they could glean their own sense of meaning, which risks incorrect interpretations and people operating at cross purposes.

NEVER LEAVE AN OPPORTUNITY ON THE TABLE TO TELL PEOPLE WHAT YOU WANT THEM TO TAKE AWAY OR HOW YOU WANT THEM TO INTERPRET SOMETHING.

There are three ways to be educational, beyond just pushing a message:

- **Widen the aperture.** It's important that leaders communicate context and help people see the bigger picture. Connect the dots and help people see how one thing relates to another or is part of a long-term plan. This is educational and can also be inspiring. Help people see how their daily work, or the project at hand, relates to a broader trend or a broader body of work.

- **Define your terms.** Keep jargon and acronyms to a minimum. Even within an organization, terms of art or jargon are defined differently in different places. You'd be surprised how many people have different understandings of the same basic terms. Tell people how you want them to define them, and what you mean by a term. Don't leave this opportunity to bring people with you on the table.

- **So what?** It's up to you to define and explain the consequences or outcomes you want people to understand.

Don't assume everybody's takeaways are the same. Tell them why it matters and what you want them to leave with.

There's a learning opportunity in each presentation and communication. One consulting client I worked with recently was focused entirely on educating the employee population about the work of their security team—to make sure people knew how the team was keeping them and their users safe. It resulted in increased satisfaction scores for the team and more knowledge around the company about how all the different teams' work fit together.

It was important because it was core to the company mission, but also it had the effect of really inspiring and motivating other employees around the company. People love knowing the stories behind the context in which they operate and are more apt to feel part of a team and give the team the benefit of the doubt when they know more about what's happening. Leaving an opportunity for simple education about a process, a moment, or a concept on the table means you're leaving a chance to connect and inspire on the table.

A WORD ON EFFECTIVE MEETINGS

Meetings are a primary communications vehicle in the workplace. Too often meetings go wrong because of a communications failure as much as because of the substance of what's being discussed. I have done a lot of education with teams and employees on how to run effective meetings—including encouraging people not to feel like they need to attend every meeting they're invited to.

50 percent of the work of a meeting is done before the meeting itself. Here are a few communication tips for organizing a successful meeting before it begins:

- **Select the right audience.** Who needs to be in the meeting? Who is running the meeting? Who is a decision-maker in the meeting? Is someone taking notes? Be clear on their purpose for being there. I like sorting the contents of meetings into two categories: *nice* to know and *need* to know.

- **Select the right timing.** Is this a regular update meeting or a one-time discussion?

- **Clarify the purpose.** What's the one reason for the meeting? Is it to check in and share regular updates? Is it to make a decision?

- **Determine and set the agenda.** What do you need to discuss to drive to the outcome? Keep this list to three or fewer items.

- **Share the agenda in advance so everyone is on the same page.** I like an agenda that is consistent over time for regular meetings and that leads to clear takeaways and action steps at the end. Good agendas include the following:

  - A clear statement of purpose for the meeting.

  - A review of (or introductions for) meeting attendees.

- A review of takeaways from previous meetings.

- Discussion. Limit the discussion to two or three substantive issues. If you have more than two or three, it limits the ability to focus in on specific issues. Consider breaking the meeting into multiple sessions to devote adequate time to each topic.

- A review of decision points and next steps.

- An opportunity for feedback or related issues to be raised.

The other 50 percent of the work of a meeting is the actual meeting. During the meeting:

- Follow the agenda. Review the entire agenda at the beginning so everyone knows where the meeting is headed, to help keep people on track and on time.

- Allow for sufficient discussion, including being aware of people on video conference or on the phone and giving space for those who are quieter or who might not speak up to be heard.

- Review next steps and action plans, including owners of action steps. This should take place during the last five minutes of the meeting.

- Allow an opportunity to ask questions and raise other issues that haven't yet been raised. I like the phrases

"What am I missing?" or *"Where am I wrong on this?"* because they actively invite feedback and an opportunity for people to share what's on their minds.

Afterward, send out a follow-up summary of the meeting. When it's in writing, it's a lot easier for everyone to understand what happened and what next steps should be. Aim for concision, using bullets, main points, and a summary of when the next meeting is and what needs to happen before then.

BEST COMMUNICATIONS PRACTICES IN HARD WORK SITUATIONS

I've seen these strategies work across the board, from big tech companies to smaller nonprofits, because they have all realized the direct correlation between healthy communication and a successful business. Some of the best practices I've seen include:

- **Writing things out.** Making writing things out a regular discipline is helpful in all kinds of ways. The author Flannery O'Connor famously said, *"I write because I don't know what I think until I read what I say."* This is true for many of us. Giving yourself the space to write out a problem will give you the chance to work through any emotions surrounding it and get to the real root of what is wrong and how to fix it. This is why therapists encourage journaling: because getting things out of your head and onto paper is a great way to reflect in a safe, nonjudgmental fashion, and will likely make your communication with others about the issue more productive. When you put pen to paper, the ideas in your head become concrete. Building the discipline of putting your ideas onto paper can force clarity and alignment and help you zero in on areas of conflict or disagreement. In the law, there's a saying that "the opinion writes itself"—which refers to the idea that, as they write opinions on complex issues, the conclusions of judges shift and evolve through the discipline of making the abstract concrete. Especially at work, if you're struggling to agree on a particular issue or project, write it out. This makes sure everyone has a chance to react and get on, well, the same page.

- **Focusing on process.** When we are invested in our work, it's only natural that we will take the results of our work personally. In some ways, this is great. We should all feel like the work we do matters and care deeply about our impact. But when conflicts arise, and they will, it's easy to let those emotions cloud our ability to problem-solve. Often we become defensive or, when presented with negative feedback, look for a problem in the person delivering the feedback. When communicating about an issue, compartmentalize and segment. Identify what is going well, what isn't, and how to fix those things. Identify and agree on the issues you're talking about, and go one by one. There are tons of books about how to navigate feedback. One I especially like is *Thanks for the Feedback* by Douglas Stone and Sheila Heen.

- **Agreeing to disagree.** No matter how much we'd love to convince everyone to see things our way, sometimes they won't. And that is okay. Being able to agree to disagree and then let the issue go is imperative to a healthy work environment. If an issue arises and you're unable to move on, then you will need to go back to the all-important task of self-reflection. What is really bothering you? Are you simply bored or frustrated you haven't gotten your way? Do you have a pattern of quitting a job in a rage every time things get hard? Know when to move on—and be careful to determine whether a sticking point is critical to moving forward in your job or just an argument you're trying to win.

- **Focusing on the bigger picture.** It is really easy to get wrapped around the axle in situations where work is challenging. It can be tempting to make gossiping and venting a part of your day, no matter how unhealthy it is to the work culture. But the most successful teams don't let this happen. They are self-aware enough to know that behind one problem at work, another one arises. At its core, your job is about problem-solving, and your career will hopefully be a long one. So focus on what matters: the relationships you're building and the path you're setting for yourself and your future.

- **Responding quickly and directly.** There's usually a golden hour right after a crisis happens, especially in a social media environment. You should immediately ask yourself: *"What would a reasonable person say here?"* And then say it. This allows you to control the narrative and be seen as honest and empathetic. If you don't know, say you don't know. But leaving charges leveled against you or against others, or silence after something goes wrong, only allows others to develop stories about you, and it's a lot harder to change people's perceptions once they're made. Balance not overreacting and not focusing too much on outrage. Being measured and thoughtful inspires confidence and empathy for your position.

- **Speaking slowly.** Especially if you're in a role where speaking is a big part of your job or you must repeat the same thing often (like a teacher, a clerk, a nurse, or a server), it's super important to discipline yourself to speak slowly so the audience hears you. You'll likely have a tendency to speak quickly because you know the recipe or the instructions by heart. But most people you're speaking to are just hearing it for the first time—and since it's not about what you say but about how they hear what you say, it's your job to make sure they are hearing you. Make it seem like you're telling each person for the first time. Turn off the autopilot and engage directly with people.

CHAPTER 5

Effective Communication in Your Personal Life

"Effective communication starts with the understanding that there is my point of view (my truth) and someone else's point of view (his truth). Rarely is there one absolute truth, so people who believe that they speak the truth are very silencing of others. When we recognize that we can see things only from our own perspective, we can share our views in a nonthreatening way. Statements of opinion are always more constructive in the first person 'I' form . . . The ability to listen is as important as the ability to speak . . . Miscommunication is always a two-way street."

—SHERYL SANDBERG

Lean In: Women, Work, and the Will to Lead

The root of all good communication is the same. The more direct and thoughtful you can be, the better—whether it's at work, at home, or anywhere in between.

We talked early on about being more aware of our internal narrative, especially when situations are challenging. One other facet of our brains that makes disagreement of any sort hard, especially when it comes to personal issues: our brains are wired for confirmation bias.

We don't like the feeling of disagreement—which can come from confrontation or from just hearing things we don't believe. And when we do enter a confrontation, we move away from a center point of shared understanding and common ground and toward the corners of "I'm right, I want to win this argument." We tighten our grasp on our narrative instead of reaching for a more objective reality.

But if you start from a place of honesty and respect, it's hard to go wrong.

For some people, this comes naturally in a work setting. They are easily able to set aside their emotions, think logically, and problem solve effectively. But in a personal setting, this can be a different story. When emotions come into play (and of course they do when it comes to the people we feel close to), it's a lot harder to think rationally and clearly. There is history to contend with, vulnerabilities that are hard to navigate, and the careful dance of wanting to be heard and understood while not hurting the ones we love—or are trying to woo.

Let me share a story I think will be familiar to many of you. Not long ago, I was starting to date someone I really liked. He was a handsome man, creative in ways I'm not, thoughtful, kind, and funny. We were spending more and more time together. He was affectionate, which felt good, and seemed interested in me and who I was. I increasingly found myself thinking about him when we weren't together, but also restraining myself from texting him and wanting to see him constantly—lest I scare him away or seem overeager.

Then, all of a sudden, he stopped returning my texts. He was increasingly distant. I started wracking my brain about what I had done or what changed. The silence led me to become concerned, but I still wanted to play it cool. I texted again, trying to get some clarity, only to get short responses.

"Hey, I'm good." No reciprocal, "How are you?" No acknowledgment of the ghosting. Silence.

Finally, a week later, the clarifying text arrived, along the lines of, "Hey, you're a great guy, you're sweet, and I love spending time with you, but I'm not looking for anything serious, and this is where I feel like this is going. I'm crazy busy with work, starting a new business myself, and don't feel like I devote the time to you that you deserve—you deserve better."

Leaving aside this person's inability to explore something more serious with me, when I looked at the situation as a communications example, two key points stood out to me:

First, the silence and ghosting felt disrespectful and hard for me to understand because my brain started imposing all kinds of stories, dramas, and explanations without any basis in reality—my emotional reactions took over, whether or not they were justified. The silence and ghosting also helped me to see that often it's uncomfortable for people to confront personal and emotional issues, let alone articulate them to others. Sometimes it's easier to say nothing, especially if you don't know exactly what to say.

Second, when he did finally tell me what was up, the actual communication was powerful because it was honest and showed respect and empathy for me and for his own feelings. It was direct and gave me clarity on where to go from there. Disappointing, to be sure. But clarity was helpful for me, almost assuredly a relief to him, and an opportunity for us both to practice being more in touch with our own emotions.

Ironically, when the stakes are highest in our personal relationships, we can find the most difficulty being direct, clear, and empathetic. We can do hard things without being hardened by them. This is hard work sometimes, but it's important work. And it starts with empathy.

CARE: A FRAMEWORK FOR COMMUNICATING WITH FAMILY AND FRIENDS

The work around communicating well in your personal life looks a whole lot like the work you do in your professional life, with one difference. Instead of CORE (consistent, open, real, and educational), the acronym we'll be working with is CARE (consistent, authentic, real, and empathetic). Not that at work you don't need to be authentic or empathetic (you do), but a foundational part of success in communicating in your personal life is taking a bit more care and being more careful.

CONSISTENT

Consistent communication with a loved one means more than scheduling regular date nights or calling your parents every Sunday. Consistent communication means building a trustful method of communicating that will withstand the test of time. We've all heard of people who haven't spoken to each other in years, but when they get back together it's like no time has passed. That's not because they forced a constant back-and-forth but because they built a trustful foundation that was easily replicated years later.

Similarly, the style of your communication with the people you're closest with (and the people you're forging new relationships with) should be consistent. When people trust that the person you are in one scenario will be the person you are in another, you're more than halfway to a healthy pattern of communication.

AUTHENTIC

Authenticity means honesty, especially in our personal relationships. The way to make sure you are communicating authentically is to check in on your motivations. When you have something important to say to someone you love, ask yourself: What result are you hoping for? The same goes for a brand-new relationship or friendship. Honesty with the other person is of course important, but honesty starts with being honest with yourself.

Think about this in terms of a family wedding. In these types of social situations, we are under so much pressure, most of it self-imposed, to present a certain image of ourselves. And to what end? If you are constantly working on your outward presentation (and that is a whole lot of energy, when you think about it), when do you have time to be your authentic, true self with the people closest to you?

Trust me, being authentic is a relief to those around you. It gives them permission to do the same.

For example, in 2018, the year Facebook added "Coming Out" as a life event option, I wrote a post about my own coming-out experience and why it was important. I wrote it to give people a bit of a fuller sense of who I am and to help create an example for more people to follow—to help others feel safe about coming out on their own too. The comments and nearly four hundred "likes" alone, as well as the numerous private messages I received from people, showed me how real authenticity can be powerful and meaningful:

I came out after being nudged out by two friends who set me up with a boy (I'm living proof you can be set up before you're out without even realizing it's a set-up)— the first boy I ever kissed, the first boy I ever allowed myself to like, the first person I uttered the words "I'm gay" to (it happened late at night over AOL instant messenger). He showed up and took me out for dinner the next night out along the coast to make sure he— the only soul who knew then—was there for me . . . and so many friends have showed up and supported me through ups and downs and in-betweens since then.

Looking back, I see what a huge relief it was, how grateful I am to have been supported where so many are not, and mostly how powerful it feels to learn to love yourself—all of yourself. I don't know if ever I'll be married, but I do know that the capacity to love and share yourself with others is a gift [. . .] one I cherish sharing with others and try to do as much as I can to allow others to do the same.

Coming out is significant because it's a moment of at last stepping into the light of love out of the darkness of fear, and it lights the way for so many others to step out of their own darkness. I wouldn't change myself for anything.

REAL

When I say real, I mean direct. Clear. Concise.

- "It hurt me when you said ____."

- "I'm feeling ____ because of ____."

- "I'm worried about you because of ____."

- "Let's talk about a way to fix ____."

Keep in mind that real, direct communication can involve what's *not* said as much as what *is*. Sometimes being real means knowing that certain topics are off-limits (political discussions at the Thanksgiving table, for example).

Establishing a pattern of real communication in your personal life can be incredibly powerful. When people can trust you'll be direct with them, you open up a whole new world of possibility with the relationship. And think about all the energy you'll conserve when you stop dancing around issues or coming at situations trying to be someone you aren't!

EMPATHETIC

I've talked a lot about empathy already, and it is particularly important to include in the personal communications framework. Empathy is the magic ingredient in every relationship. Empathy means being able to get out of your own skin for a bit and see things—really see them—from another person's point of view. This is hard sometimes, sure. And it can be especially hard in a personal context.

Let's take dating as an example. For many people, the advent of online dating has been both a blessing and a curse. It's a lot easier to summon the courage to say hi or reach out to someone if you know if they've already indicated they are interested in you. But it's also habituated the act of swiping and quickly dismissing people because there's always another match, another batch of people waiting for you. It's habituated our judging of others based primarily on their looks and what they put out into the world, rather than what we discern from getting to know them a bit more.

Let's say you're engaging in a conversation with someone and things are going well. At least you think things are going well, until you abruptly don't hear from the person. It's only natural to let your mind make up stories about what is going on, whether or not they are true:

- He's ghosting me.

- I must have done something wrong.

- This always happens. People suck!

- I'm too old. I'm not cute enough. I'm not interesting enough.

- I don't know why I bother with this thing.

- He's a jerk after all.

Certainly, one of those scenarios could be true. But you don't know that. It could be something totally different.

It could be that he's insecure and unable to simply say, "Thanks, but I'm not interested," or, "You seem great, but if I'm honest I'm not really feeling the right connection here."

You can only control how you react to the situation, and your reaction will say a lot about who you are.

HOW WE REACT TO THE WORLD AROUND US, AND HOW WE COMMUNICATE ABOUT IT, IS ENTIRELY WITHIN OUR CONTROL AND CREATES MUCH MORE OF OUR EXPERIENCE THAN OTHER PEOPLE'S ACTIONS DO.

Similarly, take the example of having to have a difficult conversation with an elderly relative, maybe a parent, about their personal safety behind the wheel. Telling them you think they should stop driving might be incredibly hard for them to hear. You have a few options:

- Say nothing. It's too hard!

- Come at it aggressively. You're clearly the one who should be in control, after all.

- Drop subtle hints and hope your relative comes to the decision to stop driving on their own.

- Call a sibling and beg them to have the hard conversation for you.

These types of difficult scenarios are part of life, and empathy is the key to handling them. Instead of thinking about how you feel about the situation, think about how the other person might be feeling.

What does empathy actually look like? It looks like giving someone the benefit of the doubt and believing that they mean well. If you go around looking for a problem, you'll find it. If you look for people who hurt your feelings, you'll find them. Empathy also means anticipating how a certain message might be received by another person. Try to really imagine how it would feel to receive your message. Empathy means thinking about all the potential underlying factors that might influence the way people react to you. Empathy is being honest and vulnerable because it's the right thing, not because you're expecting something in return. And empathy means helping the other person understand where you're coming from by being clear about your motivations and your intentions.

IF YOU WANT PEOPLE TO UNDERSTAND WHERE YOU ARE COMING FROM, BE SURE **YOU** *UNDERSTAND WHERE YOU ARE COMING FROM AND TRY TO PUT YOURSELF IN THEIR SHOES.*

Communicating in your personal life is so much about developing a connection with someone else. This might sound simple, but it can be profoundly empowering to remind yourself that it's okay to tell people how you feel and where you are coming from. Vulnerability is a good thing, and no one can read your mind.

THE POWER OF APOLOGY AND SPEAKING UP

Of course, sometimes having an open and honest discussion with people in your personal life can be really hard. That's why people avoid it so much. But it's necessary. It's essential to the health of your relationship.

I've had the great fortune of working for, working with, and hiring many excellent women in every job I've had. At Facebook, my boss was a woman, her boss was a woman, and her boss was Sheryl Sandberg. In my first two jobs on Capitol Hill as a young communications staffer, both of my bosses were women. I learned a ton from them all—not only about how to be better at communications but also about how to be a strong, empathetic leader.

Unlike some of the women I've worked with, none of these leaders apologized before or after speaking up. Too often, especially in corporate culture, women—and some men too—feel the need to apologize for having an opinion, sharing a nugget of wisdom, or simply speaking up in a meeting. Addressing the roots of this instinct to apologize regularly is beyond the scope of this book. But as a communications point, I've found it unfortunate because it undermines both the credibility of the speaker and the impact of the substance of what the person is sharing. Notice how often people apologize for asking a question, offering an idea, or simply doing their job.

GENUINE APOLOGIES—NOT THOSE SIMPLY AS A REFLEXIVE RESPONSE ROOTED IN SOME KIND OF SOCIAL ROLE OR WITHOUT EVEN THINKING WHAT YOU'RE APOLOGIZING FOR, BUT REAL APOLOGIES— ARE AN IMPORTANT MEANS OF FINDING COMMON GROUND, BUILDING TRUST AND RESPECT, AND MOVING FORWARD.

In situations where I've managed large teams and meetings, there is inevitably one person in the room who dominates the conversation and interrupts to share their views, which has the effect of silencing others. Often, it's not malicious; sometimes they don't even realize they are doing it. But in constantly dominating the conversation, they silence the speech and ideas of others.

Simply pointing it out to the person, in a respectful way, and encouraging them to apologize to those they interrupt can go a long way to building better team dynamics and getting the best out of everyone on the team. Encouraging someone to apologize can be as simple as pulling the person aside and kindly suggesting that an apology would be meaningful or setting a good example yourself and apologizing when you're in a similar situation. The same applies in a social setting—at a party, among a group of friends, or in a group of strangers. The more we do it, the easier it becomes to get over the discomfort of fear and to create meaningful connection with each other.

It should be pretty obvious that I'm a fan of apologizing when you feel you've genuinely done something wrong. If you've gotten into an argument or reflected on your own behavior and found fault, apologize! I've rarely, if ever, come across someone who has regretted apologizing when they have been at fault.

The key phrase there is "at fault." Don't apologize for the sake of shutting down a conversation or because it's expected of you. If you are always apologizing without really meaning it, as a reflexive response or for some ulterior motive like intimidating someone or silencing a conversation, your real apologies will be hollow. Apologies, like all words, lack meaning when they are given half-heartedly or with ulterior motives.

Apologies are hard, but they're a key tool you can use to take off the mask, be more truly yourself, and connect with your audience. We can all think of companies with a product recall or an advertising campaign gone awry. We can all think of politicians who did something or said something people found objectionable—or worse. In a crisis or a hard situation, an apology is a way of expressing confidence in yourself and in your relationship with your audience, and is the best way to keep a small crisis from becoming a big one.

Scandals often become scandals less for the action in question and more for how they are handled after the fact. Too often failure to apologize genuinely betrays a fake sense of self-confidence, and makes it seem like you care more about yourself and your self-perception than the other person. A direct, immediate admission of fault or failure makes people feel heard and valued and makes you seem more authentic and honest, less focused on saving face and more focused on maintaining the relationship with your audience—whether they're your constituents or your customers.

De-escalate drama and deflate a scandal by giving a full, honest, apology (and meaning it), and you'll be well on your way to mastering a key part of communication.

THE POWER OF TAKING A BREAK

Your communications with those close to you will involve big emotions, and the key to successful communications is to keep those emotions in check. You simply cannot think clearly when your emotions are in a heightened state. When your emotions are high, do yourself the favor of taking a break.

Go on a walk. Listen to some music. Give yourself the gift of time to reflect on the situation objectively and empathize with where the other person might be coming from.

This might all be stuff you already know, but in the heat of the moment, it's really hard to calmly suggest taking a walk around the block. Like any muscle, this communication practice will need to be flexed to help it grow.

How do you do this? Start by articulating this communication strategy with the people around you. Let them know to expect you to do this when emotions are high. Recognize your habits and knee-jerk reactions. This is especially important on social media, where it can be so easy to lash out and feel uninhibited by the consequences. Be aware of when you are using a lack of communication as a form of passive aggression. This is a challenge even for the best communicators; sometimes it just seems easier to avoid confrontation and maintain the status quo. Think about these times as lost opportunities for growth in your relationships. Own your reactions. Again, this goes back to the crucial work of self-reflection. Don't ever fall into the trap of blaming your reactions on someone else. You own what you put out into the world.

QUESTIONS AND PRACTICES FOR LIFE'S HARDEST SITUATIONS

It might not seem this way, but we don't communicate enough. Sure, we have thousands of channels through which to communicate with one another, and for many of us it feels like we are saturated day in and day out with news, text messages, and email. We are! But that's not the communication I'm talking about.

In fact, I think that all this one-way communication we have come to rely on makes it even more important to prioritize authentic connections with the people in our personal lives. Your social media posts will be missed or misunderstood. Your lack of response on email or to a text message could be taken any number of ways, no matter what your intentions might have been. You will have to have very hard conversations. That is life, and there is nothing we can do to avoid it.

My best advice for when those situations arise (or when you seek out these opportunities for authentic connection with the people in your life) is to come from a place of inquiry.

Be curious about the situation, and try to stand back as an impartial observer. This will allow you to be more genuine. Here are some questions you can ask yourself to help guide you:

- What do I want in this situation? What am I scared might happen? What's the worst that could happen? What's my ideal outcome?

- Am I avoiding or ignoring, and why?

- What is the other person thinking? What words would they use to describe me based on how I've been speaking and acting toward them?

- What could I say or do to show the other person that I've been respectful toward them? To make them feel heard?

- What are two or three different ways I could say the same thing?

- Have I apologized in an honest and direct way? Have I taken ownership of how I might be perceived to the other person?

The benefits of this sort of genuine self-reflection are enormous. Genuine empathy and honest dialogue are the cornerstones of any relationship, whether it's just beginning or has lasted years.

Putting these communications practices into use will, more than anything else, change the dynamics of your relationships for the better. The ramifications of this are endlessly positive for you.

CHAPTER 6

Effective Communication Using Social Media in Your Life

"If you're always trying to be normal, you'll never know how amazing you can be."
—MAYA ANGELOU

"Many can argue, not many converse."
—A. BRONSON ALCOTT

"Two monologues do not make a dialogue."
—JEFF DALY

THE SOCIAL MEDIA REVOLUTION

Technology has changed our lives rapidly, and our collective memories are short. Some of you reading this book didn't grow up with social media, smartphones, and nonstop cable news, but things have changed so much even in the last ten years that it's almost impossible to remember our lives without this constant "connection" to one another. Email barely existed when I was in college, Facebook only opened up to everyone who was above thirteen and had an email address in 2006, and the first iPhone came out in 2007. The ephemeral personal messaging app, Snapchat, started in 2011.

Our global culture's shift in what we deem to be information—and the fact that everyone now has their own publishing platform and a built-in audience—has been nothing short of a revolution. Whether broad-based audience platforms or individual messaging services, whether sharing and connecting in the town square or around the kitchen table, whether through posting a picture that will last forever or sending one that disappears after seconds, social media has changed the way we communicate, connect, empathize, and understand ourselves. And it's challenged our notions of privacy in how we communicate and share with others.

As with any revolution, there are huge growing pains and shifts to deal with. We've seen the good and bad sides of that play out in spades, especially in the last couple of years.

The first thing to remember about social media in general is that no one is forcing you to use any of these platforms. They are a powerful means for sharing, communicating, connecting, and learning—as well as intimidating, shaming, and bullying—but not the only means.

SOCIAL MEDIA PLATFORMS HAVE GIVEN A VOICE TO THOSE WHO MIGHT NOT HAVE HAD ONE OR KNOWN HOW TO USE IT BEFORE—AND, IN SO DOING, HAVE AMPLIFIED WHO WE ALREADY ARE.

I have several close friends who, even despite being supportive of me and my career as an executive at Facebook for several years, have chosen not to be on Facebook, and even more who have chosen to leave the service in recent years. I don't argue with them; it's their choice (even if it might be one I disagree with). I'd rather all of us focus on how to use any of the communications tools at our disposal to be better, fuller versions of ourselves.

There are countless examples of how social media has transformed and benefited communications, especially at work. It's made possible cultures of openness, transparency, feedback, and sharing of information that were not possible even ten years ago, and which are now the standard for most organizations globally. It has helped increase the rate at which teams can collaborate, share, and learn. It's helped people join together in various forms of community, around shared interests and work—even across oceans and time zones. Through video, photos, and technological advances that help us identify and root out bad actors, social media and the technology associated with it have been truly transformative.

Like it or not, social media is a dominant form of communicating today, both as a channel and in how it has transformed the ways we communicate—the pace, the level of formality, the size and scope of the audience, and the expectations we have of responses and reactions from others.

But how do we—individually, in all parts of our lives—have a better relationship with social media tools in a way that helps us communicate and connect with each other better, rather than becoming more estranged from each other, and the tools themselves?

It begins from the premise, like the premise of this book, that social media are communication tools—not replacements for communication.

WE HAVE COME TO OFTEN RELY ON SOCIAL MEDIA DOING THE WORK OF INTERACTING AND CONNECTING FOR US—WHEN, REALLY, WE SHOULD BE WORKING WITH IT TO HELP US INTERACT AND CONNECT.

Social media isn't, and was never, meant to be a replacement for real connection and real conversations. Interpreting a "like" or a photo as an accurate, full representation of a person's life is easy to do, but isn't what friendships and real connections are about.

Do you use social media as a tool for talking about yourself or for connecting with people, places, or topics? Is it about presentation or connection?

Social media is really wonderful in a lot of ways. It can help us learn, share, and grow. In my time at Facebook, I was witness every single day to the wonderful things social media can do: create global communities, start positive and powerful movements, keep people connected in times of crisis, and give a voice to people who might have felt voiceless. It's empowered many to talk about things they never would have before and feel connected to people they might not otherwise have connected with.

At its best, social media keeps us connected and engaged despite our busy day-to-day lives. It provides access to more information about a broader array of topics—and more knowledge generally leads to better decisions. Social media can also bring untold amounts of joy and fellowship, whether we're sharing life's most meaningful moments or our sillier, imperfect moments or rants.

But none of us has to think too hard about all the ways that the social media revolution has not been all that wonderful. People use social media as a replacement for in-person communication. (It's not.) Subtleties can be lost, and the pressure to present our "best selves" can be crushing. We often lose sight of *being* because we're too focused on *presenting* a curated version of ourselves. Social media is an additive, not a replacement. It's a tool, among many, to help facilitate connections—but ultimately, in-person connections lead to more effective communication.

Social media has changed our expectations of people, whether they be our elected officials, our friends and family, or even celebrities. We feel entitled to know the private business of everyone around us.

We have become used to immediacy at the expense of accuracy. We have shorter attention spans and demand the "quick fix" hopping on a social media site provides us. With posts, comments, photos, videos, and snaps coming at us nonstop, we've lost the ability to prioritize what's accurate and what's not, what's important and what's not. These shorter attention spans mean people are less likely to hear what you really mean. There's more skimming and scanning—and much more competition for your attention—so it's much harder to convey nuance, emotion, and meaning.

Social media also creates a powerful sense of FOMO— fear of missing out—that motivates us in how we show up in the world to others. Our tendency to compare ourselves to each other, to those we know and those we don't, affects how we communicate and engage with each other.

TO UNDERSTAND HOW TO USE AND CONSUME SOCIAL MEDIA AS AN EFFECTIVE COMMUNICATION TOOL, YOU HAVE TO THINK ABOUT IT THIS WAY: SOCIAL MEDIA AMPLIFIES HOW PEOPLE ALREADY ARE.

Social media in a nutshell, good and bad: it's quick, and some of it deletes after a while, so users have a lack of precision in how they speak, how they write, and how they read others. And certainly, their attention span for really listening is affected. Social media treats people as dispensable and becomes toxic to the patterns in our own heads about how we treat others and what we can expect from others.

Social media has the effect of exaggerating and exacerbating how people already are, both their positive and negative tendencies. It amplifies rage, insecurities, and our instinct to present a beautiful, perfect version of ourselves to the world. It's why we see hate speech spread online like we've not seen before. Social media didn't create more hate: it has simply given those who traffic in hate a bigger platform—and with it, a sense of legitimacy. It's amplified people's voices on political issues, in sharing pictures of their kids or their binge-drinking weekends. It's amplified our insecurities and need to keep up with the Joneses. But all these tendencies were already inside of us.

The good and the bad can go together. It's worth remembering both. It's a perspective, a version of reality. Like a photo, social media can take you to a place you never imagined or might never have been able to experience, which can open and expand minds—which is a good thing. But seeing the world through the lens of a camera or the small screen of a phone isn't the same thing as seeing it through the lenses of your own eyes.

So many of us easily transfer how we treat others (and ourselves) on social media to how we treat them in real life. Although the context may be different, we are wiring our brains to engage in the same behaviors both on and off the screen. Too often we get in the habit of drawing conclusions from someone's Instagram feed—as if we know that person and their circumstances, and we draw conclusions about them. But what we see is not a full, honest interpretation of a person's life.

We are still learning how to best use social media. A lot of that learning starts with understanding ourselves. People need to be more reflective and self-aware. It's the key to making sure that your relationship with social media is healthy for you and for all those who participate in it.

So, assuming you're choosing to use any of these media—Facebook, Instagram, Twitter, Reddit, Quora, or any number of dating apps—what follow are some ideas on how to use them more effectively and in a way that reduces your own anxieties.

IT IS UP TO YOU TO HAVE THE SELF-AWARENESS TO CONTROL YOUR USAGE, THE AMOUNT YOU SHARE, WHAT YOU SHARE, AND HOW YOU CONSUME INFORMATION FROM OTHER PEOPLE.

We need to take more ownership over what we see and why we are engaging with it. Social media is the story we tell ourselves based on what we see of others and what we think we want people to see.

This is where all the self-scientific behavior we've talked about comes into play. Being authentic in your work life can and should translate into your communications on social media. It's all connected.

Now that the negative byproducts of social media have become clear (addiction and fake news, to name a couple), it can be really tempting to think that quitting social media altogether is the answer. But that's not what I'm saying at all. Social media is a great way to stay connected to people, share, and get involved. And it's a really important tool for many businesses to reach customers in ways that are good for both parties.

What I am saying is that all the work you should be doing in your work and personal life—all the work around reflection, brevity, and understanding your audience—applies here.

Ultimately, this is about building more resilience and authenticity. With social media, we've lost the ability to read others, which is at the root of all good communications. Anyone who knows about executive presence—how people perceive you as a leader—will tell you that your ability to read others and read a room in order to modulate your behavior is at the core of the gravitas and empathy you want in a good leader.

Social media is a great tool, and it's up to us to use that tool for good.

IT'S NOT ABOUT YOU, IT'S ABOUT YOUR FOLLOWERS

It might seem counterintuitive to authenticity to think that your followers should come first. But the key to using social media effectively is to focus on the "social." As a media, it's premised on connection and linkages between and among us. We need to take responsibility for what we're putting out into the world.

We see it all the time from people with large platforms on social media: videos or "inspirational" Instagram accounts touting the importance of doing what serves you and not giving a damn what anyone else thinks.

On a certain level, this resonates with me too. The entire first part of this book has been about being more in touch with yourself so you can share it more clearly and authentically with others. And you absolutely shouldn't allow what other people think of you to dictate your life.

But the truth is that with social media—the tool—you have a platform. Whether you have one follower or ten thousand, the concept is the same: what you post will have an impact on the people reading and seeing it. It is up to you to be a responsible owner of your content on social media.

This book is about leaders. You don't have to be a CEO of a company to be a "leader." You are a leader by example. Assuming ownership over your use of social media is a key part of being a good leader.

Being thoughtful about what you post on social media, as well as how you respond to others, is the most important step in this. For some people, this will mean posting more. For some, it will mean posting less.

Whatever it is for you, remember the golden rule of this book: it is all about how you are perceived. It matters what people hear. Be respectful, honest, and thoughtful about how you come across, and your messages have a chance to resonate far beyond "likes" and comments.

A HEALTHY APPROACH TO SOCIAL MEDIA

Do you have a friend who always posts something like "Ugh" or "Super excited for tomorrow!" without any additional context? It's clearly begging for a comment, question, or validation—for attention. Or consider this example: You're at a restaurant for dinner. There's a family sitting next to you. Instead of talking about their days, their kids are staring at their phones (and likely, their parents are too). Or you're on vacation hiking in the mountains to one of the wonders of the world, and at the top you see people turned with their backs to the spectacular the view, gripping a selfie stick looking at themselves in the small screen of their phone. Does any of this sound familiar?

The proliferation of smartphones and social media has led us to a place where we spend less time interacting with the people we are closest to and are more concerned with the people we see on social media—who we may or may not even know in real life. We're losing the ability to communicate effectively because we're spending so much time engaging in the more ephemeral world of social media.

The first step toward a healthy relationship with social media both at work and in your personal life is to embrace it as a publishing platform. Think of it as a way to engage in a conversation with your followers. The tools have evolved, and social media is becoming less about perfect curation and more about authentic engagement with community. This is really good news. It requires coming to terms with both your own way of engaging with others socially and with creating boundaries and a framework for when and how you engage with social media so it doesn't become overwhelming.

The word that should be at the forefront of all your social media interactions is *purpose*. What's the reason you're posting or sharing or engaging? Nothing you say or do on social media should be something you wouldn't say or do in person.

This means you shouldn't write posts as though you're suddenly everyone's "breaking news" source. (Let's leave that to the actual news sources—and even they could refine the terms of what's actually breaking!) It means that before you post anything—anything—think about whether or not it has some value. Even if it's a picture on your Instagram story, which will disappear in a day, just do yourself the favor of being clear on why you're sharing it.

Of course, this means you won't be posting the same things across multiple platforms. The messages you post on LinkedIn versus a dating app will of course be different. But the essential "you" should be there on both platforms. Before you post in any context, you should be thinking about whether or not your post will be appreciated by those receiving it.

The second step is to have boundaries. Being a participant on social media means having a clear idea of who you are, what you want to accomplish, and how you can use the tool to help you reach that purpose. It means being aware of how you use it. Products like the iPhone and platforms like Instagram now track the time you spend on social media—and that awareness can be an important first step in noticing how much passive time you spend scrolling versus active time you spend engaging.

Your boundaries should be unique to you, but could include any of the following:

- No smartphones in the bedroom or at the dinner table. I have friends who, when they go out for dinner, stack everyone's phones in the middle of the table facedown. The first person to have to check their phone pays for everybody's dinner.

- No "friending" people you work with. This is a personal decision, but keeping some kinds of boundaries about who you interact with and how—just like you would in any other interaction in life—is healthy and made super easy on social media.

- "Unfriending" or unfollowing people who trigger you. Don't follow a bunch of shirtless models if they give you anxiety about your body or politicians if they post opinions that get you riled up.

- Refuse to engage with certain platforms (no matter how much your friends pressure you!). Each platform is a choice, not the means of interacting.

- Engage with people via these platforms as though you were having an in-person conversation. It's a lot easier to be a total asshole to someone you've never met via a screen or a text window than it is face-to-face. And the more you interact through a screen, the more you habituate that way of acting—and it shows up in other interactions in our lives.

When you're coming from a healthy place, the content will be easy. It will be effortless because it will be organic to you.

YOU AS A SOCIAL MEDIA PRODUCER

Training new yoga teachers gives me a unique opportunity to really hone in on the importance of how we use our social media platforms. If you're not a yogi, hop over to Instagram and search "#yoga" to see what I mean. Instagram is a haven for yoga teachers in beautiful clothes doing beautiful poses and quoting ancient texts for inspiration.

It's also a bastion of amplified insecurity.

This is really a double-edged sword. Being a yoga teacher, it might feel easy to show off your incredible balance (on a Hawaiian beach, no less!—guilty here) to fulfill a need for validation on your part. But the practice of yoga is about so much more than holding poses. And, really—how many of us get to practice yoga with a beautiful sunset behind us? The reality is, most of those photos were taken fifty times to get the perfect pose and the perfect framing with the right lighting and scenery, and in no way resemble an actual yoga practice.

When you are a producer on social media, as a yoga teacher or a parent or the CEO of a company, you need to ask yourself the same questions:

- What am I trying to do with this post? What is my purpose? Do I have a consistent point of view or goal for my social media?

- Will my audience appreciate what I'm trying to say here?

- Am I sure that what I'm saying is truthful? Would I say it in a yoga class, in a boardroom, or to my mom?

- Will I be okay if this post barely gets noticed?

Sure, this might seem like a lot of work for a meme or a picture of your kids at the pumpkin patch. But with more practice, these questions become innate. Maybe posting pictures of your family reunion is easy, but with more reflection you won't have to think twice before reposting an article you read from a trusted news source or comment on a sensitive topic. And in that way, you become a trusted source of information and perspective who will positively impact your followers.

You don't also have to do this every time you share a picture on Snapchat. The point is simply that we need to take more ownership over how we communicate and interact with others in life and be a little more thoughtful, honest, and reflective about why we're sharing what we're sharing and when.

One last point here: People crave positivity. Because we live in a time with lots of ill will, anxiety, and fear, there's a craving for positive messages, images, and interactions. This doesn't mean you should be fake or saccharine. It means be real, but be positive. Be positive in how you interact with others, and you'll have a more positive experience yourself with social media.

YOU AS A SOCIAL MEDIA CONSUMER

In addition to being really clear about who you are as a producer on social media, it's really helpful to be aware of how you consume social media yourself. What accounts do you follow? Whom do you respect and admire? What excites you on social media? What makes you feel good? What really bothers you, makes you feel insecure, or makes you roll your eyes?

If engaging in a respectful political discussion on Facebook excites you, do it. If it stresses you out, don't. Similarly, if following pages devoted to hilarious cat videos makes you happy, have at it. But if following tons of LA supermodels or people who do nothing but travel while you're hard at work amplifies your insecurities, don't follow or engage with those accounts. It is completely up to you how you use social media, so do it in the way that makes you feel the best.

You do not have to keep up with anyone else's comfort level; you are only responsible for yours.

WE NEED TO TAKE MORE OWNERSHIP OVER BOTH WHAT WE PUT OUT INTO THE WORLD AND WHAT WE ALLOW INTO OUR WORLDS.

Taking stock of your social media consumption might include any of the following steps:

- **Notice the amount of time you spend on social media.** Also take stock of the quality of time spent—whether you're being active or just passively scrolling.

- **Check your tendencies to keep up with the Joneses.** It used to be that you had to keep up with the Jones family who lived down the street. Now, there are a million Joneses we have to keep up with. You need to decide whether that's important to you. (Most of the time, it isn't and shouldn't be.)

- **Be kind to yourself.** Some people really aren't comfortable interacting on social media. That is okay. If that is you, own it!

- **Train your brain.** Set parameters around how much time you allow yourself to spend on social media, and maybe even around the profiles and organizations you follow. Consider sources and be intentional with your time.

Remember: you lead by example, and you set your own example. More purposeful use helps us reduce our anxiety, increase our ability to engage in real life, and defang the really hateful, negative parts of social media that are the worst of our cultures.

Social media is a powerful tool, but only as a way of adding to our way of engaging with other people in real life—even if it means spending less time on it. The key aspects of self-reflection, knowing your audience, and being clear on your purpose that we covered earlier are relevant here. Social media should be a tool, not a replacement. Taking more responsibility for what you put out through it, as well as what you allow into your life through it, will help you have a better, healthy relationship with social media and leverage all its power for something better and more rewarding.

PART 3:

Communication Tools and Conclusion

CHAPTER 7

Concluding with a Communications Toolkit for Everybody

W̶e have covered communications challenges in three main contexts—professional life, personal life, and on social media. Now, to conclude, I'll share some guidance on a few instances that cut across all three contexts.

PERSONAL NARRATIVE

In professional contexts and increasingly in personal ones, especially social media and dating sites, it's become important to have a personal narrative. In a time of Instagram, Facebook, and YouTube, younger generations are becoming really good at developing a personal brand or a personal narrative. It's something that's required of everybody, because of how we consume and share information about others.

If being brief and direct and knowing your audience are key to communication, and if the first part of all communication is looking more within yourself than outwardly toward others, then it stands to reason that a personal narrative would be at the foundation of how we communicate. It undergirds every way we interact with others in any context. How we think of ourselves and present ourselves can make us compelling for a new job or attractive to a new partner, and it can confirm—or run afoul of—people's perceptions of us.

It's often uncomfortable for people to talk about themselves because they feel boastful and self-promotional. (Although, some people really *are* too self-promotional and don't understand that there's a more interesting story to be told that's obscured by their boasting.) Despite the discomfort, it's critical today. It's also really important to be able to talk about yourself in a way that feels authentic and gets across the key aspects of yourself in certain contexts. Increasingly, how we find partners, jobs, and the homes we live in depends on our having a true narrative to share about ourselves that others find compelling and attractive.

Most importantly, make sure that your narrative matches both reality and what you put on professional networking sites and dating apps. Never lie about yourself. But keep in mind—you are much more than the sum of your experiences and accomplishments. You are how you feel, how you show up, and what you do based on those experiences.

Going one step further in drawing conclusions and weaving a story about your experiences for your potential partner or manager helps them get a better sense of who you are. Experiences grouped together by theme or by learning are way more effective than a long list of jobs and company names.

Creating a narrative out of a handful of experiences requires that you answer a couple of questions: What are the one or two common aspects of all the different jobs you've had? In one or two sentences, what motivated the moves and decisions you've made that led you to this point?

For example, I have a pretty diverse professional background—I studied political science and international security in college but had been really interested in journalism; I worked in political communications and then went to law school; in law school I focused on policy and government more than the traditional practice of law; after law school I worked at a foundation and then a nonprofit and taught a college course on nonprofits and advocacy. When I talk about my own narrative at work, the two common threads I point out through those experiences are that I have become good at distilling complex ideas in simple ways for different audiences, and I've always focused on being a good manager and leader.

Focusing less on the job title and more on what you learned in each job and their similarities helps develop a common thread through various experiences. Focusing less on providing a chronological list of actions or accomplishments and more on a theme or two that unites them is more compelling and often comes across less as bragging—and is therefore more comfortable for us to share. Do not name-drop as much as you talk about substance. Degrees, institutions, and names matter far less than what you've done and who you are.

Ask yourself: *"What is the common thread through all my experiences?"* Rather than listing a chronology of jobs and titles, tell a story about what you learned that might be relevant to someone else in each job. Talk about passions, interests, and patterns more than accomplishments. Rather than *"I worked at X and invented the first Y, and then I worked at A and built the first B,"* say *"When I worked at X creating Y, I learned the importance of Z, and at A working on B, I learned C—and Z and C led me to where I am today."*

Have a short, medium, and longer version of the same narrative. Start by creating the longer version, and then cut. Boil it down to its essence—what are the one, two, or three points that you think really encapsulate you and your experience? If you keep those as your north star, you'll always be able to run through them in a thirty-second conversation at a cocktail party, in a two-minute talk on a panel, or during a longer-form interview.

A few tips on creating a narrative or story about yourself:

- Ask for specific feedback from people you trust.

- Keep it short and direct. Don't feel the need to list every accomplishment.

- Never say something that's untrue. Ever. Only take credit for your own work.

- Don't lose an opportunity to be open, honest, and a little vulnerable. Trying to appear perfect or hide imperfections makes you seem insecure and unrelatable. We all have flaws, and it makes your narrative unrealistic to go out of your way to conceal them.

- Smile. In photos on dating websites and professional networking sites, a smile conveys accessibility and confidence. Studies have shown it's a key part of executive presence and is attractive in mates.

USING YOUR NARRATIVE:
POWERFUL DIALOGUE IN A JOB INTERVIEW

So now you've developed a narrative. But rarely is a narrative used in a one-way manner. Usually it comes up in a dialogue—commonly in a job interview. The reason to have a good narrative you feel comfortable with is that you can fall back on it when you get nervous—so when you don't know what to say or how to say it, you at least feel comfortable telling a story with a couple good facts about yourself that are relevant in the moment.

Often, we don't know exactly how to balance being too modest with being too arrogant. But we all want to share the best versions of ourselves when we are interviewing for a job. This chart has a few examples of what people commonly struggle with and a way of tweaking the wording to make it feel more positive and more comfortable. Notice as you read that the focus is more on presenting a positive perspective and not listening to the negative self-talk.

INSTEAD OF/TRY THIS:
POWERFUL DIALOGUE IN A JOB INTERVIEW

INSTEAD OF	TRY THIS
"I'm not great at X, Y, and Z. I think it's because I've never been properly trained in those things."	*"X, Y, and Z have been challenges I've liked working through in my career."*
"I basically ran the whole account team. I was in charge of W, X, Y, and Z. Here's a list of all the things I did."	*"My role was to coordinate the logistics between the Asia and North America teams for X account."*
"When I first graduated from college, I worked for X Company. Then I worked for Y Company. Then I moved to Z Company."	*"I've always gravitated toward a role in sales, and that's because I love to help customers understand how products can help them."*
"I won an achievement award from my team in 2015 for innovation."	*"My passion is innovation. My favorite thing to do is take a problem and come up with an innovative solution to solve it. For example . . ."*
"Have you ever heard of so-and-so? He's pretty famous in our field. I used to work with him."	*"I've been so lucky to learn from some great minds in this field. I love applying what I've learned at new companies."*
"I'm an introvert—sorry!"	*"I'm an introvert. I love working hard but really value my downtime."*
"I don't think I have anything about me that's interesting. I'm kind of boring!"	*"The thing I'm most passionate about outside work is yoga. I try to make time for it several times a week. It helps keep me sane!"*

SIX STEPS TO MAKE DIFFICULT
CONVERSATIONS MORE EFFECTIVE

Although we dislike conflict, we all need to have the hard but important emotional conversations. Often these conversations cut across the contexts of work, home, and social media, and they often come up because there's been a lack of good communication to start. There might be misaligned expectations or a lack of transparency or honesty. Or perhaps one or both people haven't been honest and self-reflective enough in the first instance.

When emotions run high, our brain's fight-or-flight instinct kicks in. Our brains move almost instantaneously from input to emotional response to crafting a story about that input to reaction or action. The keys are to level up our brain's response, to craft a reaction that's based more on a shared pool of facts and goals, to make the conversations more productive, and to foster the growth of relationships over time. Regardless of the context, at work or at home, difficult conversations can be navigated by using these simple steps:

1. **Start with your motivations.** Ask yourself: What do you really want? What do you really fear? What's really bothering you? Positive motivations are learning, finding truth, getting results, and cultivating connection. Negative motivations are trying to win, to be right, to blame or punish or embarrass, or to avoid. Ask yourself why this is a conversation that's important and hard to have.

2. **Recognize your own narrative.** Every person's brain develops their own narrative or story about a person or situation. We all carry these around with us. Recognize

and know yours. Separate out the facts from opinions, and see how what you see or hear immediately turns into a story, which immediately turns into a feeling that then drives how you act. Separating facts helps clarify your own narrative. Are you seeing yourself as a protagonist or an antagonist? As a victim or a villain? Positive motivations are rooted in facts and shared understanding; negative motivations are rooted in stories, assumptions, and narratives about other people and situations (which often aren't realistic).

3. **Make it feel safe for others.** Start from a place of respect. Make sure to clarify your intent and your connection with the other person. Prioritize that connection over content. People get defensive when they perceive negative intent. Notice if someone is being silent or violent—this is when you're being less persuasive and more abrasive. Silence and avoidance only make things worse. Communication from a place of positive intent allows you to talk through and work through your narratives.

4. **Acknowledge the narratives.** State the facts, share your narrative, ask about others' narratives, and then converse with the other person. Ask about their story and their assumptions, and then explore rather than expounding.

5. **Make it feel safe for them to share with you and explore their paths.** Make it your goal to understand their point of view. Don't react right away. When you

do, you can find where the narratives don't match up and talk through the differences. Thank them for the feedback and for sharing something hard, and mean it. Express gratitude and admiration for what's going well. Positive feedback is important.

6. **Clarify action and outcomes:** Who does what? When? What is a next step? Even if you agree to disagree, what will you do differently? How do you move forward?

Notice that the point of actually sharing the content itself doesn't happen until step five. Laying the groundwork, focused on connection, trust, empathy, and understanding your own narrative and purpose, comes first. Having these types of conversations from an honest place, with the intention not just of venting but of being heard, means also making sure the other person feels heard, seen, and acknowledged. It's about finding the overlap in the different narratives or interpretations we all carry around in our heads.

TWENTY-FIVE HABITS OF EXCELLENT COMMUNICATORS

Good communicators work at it. They develop good habits and patterns that reflect clarity of purpose, empathy, and care, and they are thoughtful about how and what they say. Much like an Olympic athlete or a concert musician practices and hones their skill with drills so that the basics become habits, so too with communication. This book has covered a lot of ground and given a lot of advice. But the following tips have risen to the top again and again over time, in many conversations and contexts, languages, and demographics. In my experience, these are the twenty-five habits that go into making an excellent communicator:

1. **They carefully check for grammar and spelling errors before they send emails, texts, and posts on social media.** It might seem like I'm nitpicking here, but it's true what your fifth-grade teacher always said: your spelling and grammar matter. This of course doesn't mean that you will always be perfect; typos happen. But this comes back to the idea of care and conscientiousness in your communication. It's about being perceived how you want to be perceived—as thoughtful, credible, and intentional. Again, it's about the audience, not you. You might have the most important idea in the history of your company, but if you send an email riddled with errors, it will show to the recipient that you didn't put a whole lot of thought into relaying the message— which makes it seem like you don't really care about them. Especially if you're a communications professional, you should try to communicate clearly and effectively and set a good example.

2. **They are direct.** Excellent communicators don't beat around the bush. They don't couch difficult news in fluff. They don't leave people guessing as to their true intentions. They say exactly what they mean directly. Just come out and say it.

3. **They are genuinely empathetic.** If there's one tool we can all work on to make the world a better place, it's empathy. When a person feels heard and understood, they are more likely to listen to what you have to say, and your work together (both professtional and personal) will be much more fulfilling. Be respectful and get out of your own way.

4. **They find a true connection with people.** Have you ever met someone who made you feel as though you'd been friends or colleagues forever? This isn't divine intervention; this is one person's ability to find what connects them to others and make the most of it.

5. **They are good storytellers.** Some of the best communicators understand the basics of ninth-grade English: a story must be compelling in order to captivate the hearts and minds of your audience. Whether you're talking about the challenges of a certain project or having a conversation with someone in your personal life, the best way to be heard is to tell a good story. A good story can be an example, a short narrative, or something more imaginative. It's how good communicators move from telling to showing.

6. **They use body language well.** Good communicators maintain eye contact with the people they are talking to. They shake hands confidently and don't cross their arms while being spoken to. These might seem like small things, but the way you present yourself

physically can make a huge impact in terms of how much you're understood and heard.

7. **They are constantly referring back to the mission, the goal, or the shared connection.** It is easy to get bogged down with the minutiae of your day-to-day operations, be it at home or at work. Great communicators are always referring back to the shared dream, whether a company mission statement or their marriage vows. Keeping your eye on the ball ensures that people are focused not just on tasks, but the greater success of your work or life as a whole.

8. **They are able to say things multiple ways.** Everyone has their own preferred method of communication, and the best communicators understand that. They don't just communicate in the way that works best for them; they find ways to make their message heard in multiple ways.

9. **They are not didactic or condescending.** One of the easiest ways to lose an audience, either at work or at home, is to either talk over or talk down to them. Great communicators talk about complicated issues in a way their audience will understand, without being preachy or making the audience feel dumb, and make sure they are bringing their audience with them.

10. **They are humble.** Think about some of the greatest minds of our generation—are they always talking about how great they are? Do they make a point of mentioning that they are extremely intelligent or

successful? Do they claim to be entirely self-made? No. The best leaders are confident, communicate gratitude, apologize honestly, and are humble about their successes, along with always looking for ways to improve. This makes them relatable and trustworthy.

11. **They make a clear distinction between facts and opinions.** Phrases like, "In my experience" or "According to the research I've read" go a very long way. Again, this goes back to trust. If your audience can trust that you're a reliable source of information, they are far more likely to trust you. Especially in our current political climate, leaders can stand out if they are clear about what's opinion and what's fact and provide a shared basis for conversation around a common set of facts.

12. **They ask questions.** Questions are incredibly powerful. Not only do they clarify a situation, but they show you are a thoughtful and careful listener. Asking questions shows that you're listening, and listening is the key to open and honest communication.

13. **They follow up when they say they will and don't leave people hanging.** You know that person in your life who takes forever to respond to a text or email? Or worse, that person who promises to follow up by a certain point and then never does? This is not just an annoyance—this is a healthy communication destroyer.

14. **They talk about their accomplishments in the context of what they learned.** This is particularly

important in a high-stakes situation, like a job interview, or if you have a hard time talking about yourself in a professional context. You absolutely should talk about all the great things you've done, but rather than supplying a list of all your accomplishments, you should be framing those accomplishments with the lessons you learned on the way. This shows humility, but it also shows a willingness and openness to learning new things.

15. **They are who they are. Always.** We've talked a lot about authenticity in this book because it really is that important. The best communicators are trustworthy in the eyes of the people they are communicating with, and that trust starts with not making people guess what version of you will show up in any given moment. Don't try to be someone you're not, because you'll likely fail every time.

16. **They are willing to have—and are good at having—difficult conversations.** We live in a culture of deflection and avoidance. Passive-aggressive behavior is the enemy of healthy communication. Great communicators are willing to have honest conversations, even when it's hard, and they do so by making sure the other person understands their motivations and intentions.

17. **They show how they feel instead of just telling.** "Show, don't tell" is one of the first rules of writing for a reason. Instead of just telling people you're upset,

showing them why with examples is much more effective.

18. **They know their audience.** Great communicators take the time to know who they're speaking to and how they will best understand information.

19. **They apologize genuinely when they've done something wrong.** "I'm sorry, but" is not what I'm referring to. A genuine apology involves reflection and ownership. The best communicators do this and also reap the benefit of stopping a story before it spins out of control in the mind of another person (or group of people).

20. **They communicate enthusiasm and passion.** Everyone is operating with their own ideals and priorities. You should care the most about what impacts you, and if you're sharing something that's really exciting or important to you that you think the audience might not know about, don't miss an opportunity to share your enthusiasm and passion. If you're not excited about what you're saying, you can't expect anyone else to be.

21. **They don't make things up.** This might sound obvious (it should be!) but sometimes a quick "white lie" about an accomplishment or motivation, or even an excuse to not go out on a date with someone, can have disastrous consequences. Honesty is always the best policy.

22. **They are the same person online as they are in real life.** Sure, you'll have some differences based on the platform (your Facebook posts might look different than your LinkedIn posts, for example), but they shouldn't be that different.

23. **They respect other people's time, energy, and privacy.** This should go without saying, but particularly in the age of social media it bears repeating:
    a. Emails should be short, succinct, and used sparingly. "Reply All" is often unnecessary.
    b. Never text or message someone with something that might be interpreted as urgent when it's not. (For example, saying "give me a call" without any additional context.) This goes back to direct communication; if less is more (and it is!) then use your words to state what you want to state as opposed to making someone guess what you want. Do people the courtesy of allowing them to prioritize.
    c. Don't overshare. This is a fine line and really depends on your comfort level. Just keep in mind that in posts on social media, texts with friends, or even lunchtime conversations with colleagues, you really don't need to tell everyone every single detail.
    d. Don't tag people on social media or call them out (particularly in regards to posting pictures) without their consent. This gets annoying fast and can definitely feel like a violation of trust.

24. **They are respectful overall.** They are respectful of themselves, of those they are talking to, of the medium,

of the time, and of the content. It's not about the communicator as much as it's about everything and everyone else.

25. **They acknowledge there is always work to be done to be a better communicator.** Being great at communication means understanding that it's a never-ending, multi-laned street. Some days you will simply be better at this than others, and that is okay. The goal isn't to be perfect all the time, it's to be conscientious all the time.

HONESTLY SPEAKING

Taking a step back, this book is as much about communications as it is about how you more fully show up in the world. And communicating is how we show up and engage with others.

In a world, and at a time, where the pace of communications is greater than ever; the volume of information, opinions, and rage is deeper; and the means of communications are more fully accessible to many, we all have a need and a desire to connect with others as a way of countering the polarization and negativity that infect our world.

And it starts with us. Words have to matter. The way we use those words has to matter. Because it's how we get the ideas and emotions and feelings inside us out, and how we understand the ideas, emotions, and feelings of others around us. Honesty has to matter.

With a bit more effort, thought, and willingness to look inside ourselves, communication challenges can be easily overcome by all of us. First, it starts with the core human idea that we all want to be heard and acknowledged. So many communications challenges arise when there's a disconnect here. To overcome them requires looking inside ourselves, understanding our own narratives and where we begin. It requires understanding our audience and putting them first—after all, it matters not what you say but what people hear. It requires listening more—more fully, more skillfully, and more deeply—to better understand what people are hearing and feeling and to make sure we can fully understand our audience, so we can all help make sure people feel heard and acknowledged. It requires different, but related, tactics for different settings—and so we talked about the unique challenges and ideas for communicating at work, at home, and on social media.

But it all comes down to three core lessons worth pondering here:

Look inside yourself first. So many religious and spiritual traditions and so many disciplines teach us about controlling our own thoughts, words, and actions as a means of reducing our suffering and creating more harmony with others in the world. The more we look inside ourselves and understand ourselves, even just a little bit, the better we will all be at communicating, especially when we doubt one another, don't understand one another, and don't feel heard by one another.

Less is more. As *The Living Gita* says, "Speak sparingly. A word is bird. Once you let it out, you can't whistle it back. Measure your words. Think that every word is a dollar and once it goes out, it won't return. Think two or three times before speaking. Let people know that you really mean what you say when you speak. People often say, 'I don't know, do you know what I mean?' Such talking creates confusion. If you think well before you utter a word, then you can convey so much with fewer words. With less energy, you perform a better job."

As we think and speak, so we become. We take on the qualities of what we talk about. Because communications is so closely linked to our own experience in every respect, what we keep in our brain and how we use it as a tool is critical. So if we are always talking about other people's problems, then we will be filled with problems. If we don't see the best in people or are constantly thinking terrible things about them, it carves deeper and deeper habitual grooves to find the worst in others. Too seldom do we praise others. The more we talk and think about bad things, the more we become bad things ourselves. It's unsafe and unhealthy to be constantly speaking ill of others. Everybody has a little weakness, but if we keep talking about that weakness, that's ultimately what we become. So we speak of the positive, or we think of things with clarity and judgment, so that we don't color every way we communicate with the same negativity and judgment we find bad in others. Good communication, with yourself and with those around you, ultimately just comes down to speaking honestly.

HONESTLY SPEAKING:
A CHEAT SHEET

The chart that follows is a tool you can use to reflect on and prepare for communicating in a variety of contexts. It's a self-reflection exercise and a preparation tool.

Use it by first remembering a few key communications points:

- Communicating is a two-way enterprise about information-sharing and relationship-building.

- It matters less what you say, more what people hear.

- Reflecting on your motivations and intentions means others are more likely to be receptive to your ideas, thoughts, and feelings.

- Am I in a proactive or reactive situation? Am I making an announcement, or am I responding to an external situation or something that's already happened?

Next, identify the situation you're in and use the chart that follows to answer as clearly and briefly as you can in each column. If one doesn't feel relevant, you can leave it blank.

Finally, after you've used it a few times in different contexts, reflect on what similarities and trends you notice in how you communicate and in what changes you might want to make.

AUDIENCE: *Who is my audience? What do they know about me and this situation? How are they approaching this interaction?*	
GOAL: *What is my goal or purpose? What do I want the outcome to be?*	
MOTIVATION: *What is my motivation for communicating this now? Why is this important?*	
CHALLENGE: *What makes it hard?*	

TONE: *What tone do I want to strike?*	
MESSAGE: *What is the content or message? (Summarize the point of what you're conveying in one sentence.)*	
WHERE: *Is this best done in writing or in person?*	
ACTION: *What action or follow-up do I need to plan or does the other person need to plan (if any)?*	

POSSIBLE SITUATIONS FOR CHART USE

- Work email

- Work presentation

- Team meeting

- 1:1 meeting

- Work presentation

- Job interview

- Family conversations or holidays

- Friends hanging out or conversation

- Dating interaction

- Partner conversation

- Interaction with strangers or customers

- Student-teacher or teacher-student conversation

RECOMMENDED READING

Interpersonal Communication and Listening

- *The Lost Art of Listening: How Learning to Listen Can Improve Relationships* by Michael Nichols
- *Crucial Conversations: Tools for Talking When Stakes Are High* by Kerry Patterson, Joseph Grenny, Ron McMillan, and Al Switzler
- *Thanks for the Feedback: The Science and Art of Receiving Feedback Well* by Douglas Stone and Sheila Heen

Effective Writing and Communication

- *Dreyer's English: An Utterly Correct Guide to Clarity and Style* by Benjamin Dreyer
- *Merriam-Webster's Dictionary of English Usage*

Knowing Your Audience and Building Connection with Others

- *Change Your Questions, Change Your Life: 12 Powerful Tools for Leadership, Coaching, and Life* by Marilee Adams
- *Radical Candor: Be a Kick-Ass Boss without Losing Your Humanity* by Kim Scott
- *Learning in Relationship: Foundations for Personal and Professional Success* by Ronald Short

Leadership Development and Culture

- *Daring Greatly: How the Courage to be Vulnerable Transforms the Way We Live, Love, Parent, and Lead* by Brené Brown
- *Good to Great: Why Some Companies Make the Leap . . . and Others Don't* by Jim Collins
- *Peak: How Great Companies Get Their Mojo* from Maslow Chip Conley
- *Give and Take: Why Helping Others Drives Our Success* by Adam Grant
- *The 100-Year Life: Living and Working in an Age of Longevity* by Lynda Gratton and Andrew Scott
- *This is Now Your Company: A Culture Carrier's Manifesto* by Mike Rognlien
- *Lean In: Women, Work, and the Will to Lead* by Sheryl Sandberg

Self-Reflection

- *Buddhism without Beliefs: A Contemporary Guide to Awakening* by Stephen Batchelor
- *How to Meditate: A Practical Guide to Making Friends with Your Mind* by Pema Chödrön
- *Buddha's Brain: The Practical Neuroscience of Happiness, Love, and Wisdom* by Rick Hanson
- *The Living Gita: The Complete Bhagavad Gita—A Commentary for Modern Readers* by Sri Swami Satchidananda
- *Zen Mind, Beginner's Mind: Informal Talks on Zen Meditation and Practice* by Shunryu Suzuki

INDEX OF RESOURCES

ACKNOWLEDGMENTS

Writing this book has been a labor of love and the result of much learning and collaboration over the years—as much about the world around me as about myself. We should all be so lucky to have a family of friends, colleagues, and mentors from whom we learn and grow, and I am blessed to have a big one in my life.

First, many friends and colleagues have indulged conversations about work, yoga, or some crazy idea or another and commiserated, debated, and laughed along the way. For this project, I'm especially grateful to Jill Greenberg, Tom Kober, Mike Rognlien, and Joe Sandillo, who helped shape and focus the content included this book, and to Andrew Urankar and Cheryl Kovalchik for their helpful feedback, edits, and suggested reframing of some key concepts here. They are the type of go-to friends who speak honestly, listen well, share thoughtfully, and are constant learners and unwavering supporters.

I'm indebted to my teachers, so many of whom have taught me about how to communicate, lead, love, and live in many contexts with strength and humility. There are too many to name all of them here, but a few especially influenced the learnings shared here: my elementary school teachers Linda Warner and Barbara Kobrin, who taught me the joy of learning and reading; Jamie Meyer, in whose high school Latin classes I learned more about English than I did from anyone else; Jim Hosney, who taught me a love of literature, style, clear and colorful communication, and passion; Professor Adrienne Jamieson, who made possible my first communications jobs in Washington and years later encouraged me to teach at Stanford in Washington about the power of advocacy and communications in politics; former Stanford Law School dean Kathleen Sullivan, my constitutional law professor, from whom I learned so much about not only our legal system but how to make a persuasive, well-reasoned, elegantly articulated argument that is heard by your intended audience; and Jason Crandell, Stephanie Snyder, Janet Stone, and Rusty Wells—each of whom shares their leadership and life lessons through the practice, studentship, and teaching of yoga. I have learned so much from them about how to communicate from a self-reflective, compassionate place and to lead a life of meaning.

I'm indebted to those who have given me the chance to practice what I've learned about communications. I'm especially grateful for those I've had the privilege to work for and learn from, and who trusted me to support them in their communication efforts along the way. Each of them reminds me about the higher calling that is being of service to others: Governor Gavin Newsom, US Senator Ron Wyden, US Representative Josh Gottheimer, former US Representative Jim Turner, former Los Angeles Mayor Richard Riordan, Mark Zuckerberg, Sheryl Sandberg, Mike Buckley, Lori Goler, Elizabeth Hurley-Burks, Josh Kardon, Tara McGuiness, Molly McUsic, Jennifer Palmieri, Elliot Schrage, Neera Tanden, and Bertie Thomson.

I've learned much about leadership and communications in practice from some very talented colleagues. From the Facebook communications team—one of the best in the business—and the Facebook people team to the small but hearty band of us in the Clinton White House Speechwriting office back in 2000, I've been fortunate to work and learn from some of the best. Many of the practical lessons shared in this book come from a result of our working together and simply just talking together along the way. A few colleagues especially deserve thanks here: Tucker Bounds, April Carson, Netta Conyers-Haynes, Carol Guthrie, Lori Lodes, Jonny Oser, Keith Rabois, Jackie Rooney, Anna Soellner, and Karen Wickre.

In terms of getting this particular book done, I'm indebted to Roseanne Cheng, one of the best writing coaches, friends, and therapy-session buddies one could ever ask for. Thank you to the Wise Ink team, who guided, designed, collaborated, edited, and made this book possible: Dara Beevas, Patrick Maloney, and Cole Nelson.

And finally, I could not have written a book about communication, leadership, love, and living without Chip Blacker, my professor, honors thesis advisor, mentor, and friend, and his husband Louie Olave, from whom I have learned so much, with whom I have been on some of life's great adventures, and to whom I offer only love and gratitude.

ABOUT THE AUTHOR

Andrew Blotky is a writer, executive coach, and expert in leadership and communications. He is the founder and CEO of Azure Leadership Group, a consultancy and coaching practice focused on leadership, communications, and culture for a variety of for-profit and nonprofit organizations worldwide. From 2013 to 2018, Andrew led employee communications globally at Facebook, where he was a leader of the company's open culture and responsible for communicating with the employees and leaders on every initiative and program across all of Facebook's platforms.

Andrew started his communications career in politics, as an intern in the White House Office of Presidential Speechwriting, and later as a communications leader for various elected officials in the US House, US Senate, and San Francisco Mayor's Office. Before joining Facebook, he built and led the legal policy and communications program at the Center for American Progress, where he partnered with the Obama Administration on building education and advocacy campaigns that focused on the US courts and judges as a political issue. He was also an adjunct professor at his alma mater, Stanford University, where he taught university courses on effective advocacy in the political process. He's also a longtime student and teacher of devotional vinyasa yoga. He lives in San Francisco, CA.

ABOUT THE TYPE

This book was typeset in Adobe Garamond, which was designed by Robert Slimbach and based on the work of French engraver Claude Garamond. It was created with the aid of fifteenth-century equipment at the Plantin-Moretus Museum.

CONTACT ANDREW

Andrew works with leaders and their teams in organizations in a variety of industries worldwide. To book him for a training or talk, or for a consulting or coaching engagement, visit:

Azure Leadership Group
www.azureleadership.com
Communications, Leadership, Culture
Training, Speaking, Consulting, Coaching